POWER AND AUTHORITY
MADE SIMPLE

POWER AND AUTHORITY
MADE SIMPLE

Praying Medic

INKITY
PRESS™

Unless otherwise noted, all scripture quotations are taken from the New King James Version®. Copyright © 1982 by Thomas Nelson, Inc. Used by permission. All rights reserved.

Inkity Press™
137 East Elliot Road, #2292, Gilbert, AZ 85299

This book and other Inkity Press titles can be found at:
PrayingMedic.com

Available from Amazon.com, and other retail outlets.

For more information visit our website at **www.inkitypress.com**
or email us at **admin@inkitypress.com** or **admin@prayingmedic.com**

ISBN-13: 978-1-947968-13-4 (Inkity Press)

Printed in the U.S.A.

TO THE MEMORY OF JOHN Paul Jackson, who pioneered the modern-day effort to return to the biblical models of power and authority.

TABLE OF CONTENTS

THIS IS THE SIXTH BOOK in the series *The Kingdom of God Made Simple*. Although a late entry in the collection, it is in many respects the most fundamental of all the books in this series. If one hopes to live as a mature child of God, one must understand how to wisely wield power, and exercise authority.

In most of my books, I teach in a straightforward manner about concepts and principles related to God's kingdom. I typically describe a principle, and explain how it can be applied in everyday life. In this book, however, I will endeavor to correct doctrines that, although taught by good men and women, are nevertheless incorrect.

Much of what is taught today about power and authority doesn't reflect the way these concepts were demonstrated by Jesus and His disciples. In the last two millennia, erroneous teachings have crept into Christian theology. As a result, many believers do not experience the kind of miracles seen by the first century church. When they attempt to wield power or authority, and experience poor results, it demonstrates a flawed understanding of these twin pillars of the kingdom. My intent is to provide readers with the information they need to use power wisely and exercise authority the way God intended. That will require a bit of correction regarding some popular doctrines.

The subjects discussed this book may be described using the broad category of prayer. Although I engage in prayer often, I had never analyzed the different modes of prayer, their practical applications, advantages, limitations, and common misconceptions about them. Power and authority are matters of relationship. Prayer is one way in which we relate to our Creator. I will offer observations about the ways we relate to God through prayer, and how these practices may facilitate the release of power and the exercise of authority.

Although authority can be used to calm a storm or evict a demon, it has far broader application. The believer is intended to live as God's representative on the earth. As heaven's representatives, we're authorized to carry out certain tasks and deliver certain messages. God's commission is specific to each individual. We are created to carry out a unique destiny. If you have not yet discovered your divine destiny, the later chapters of this book will explore that subject.

~ Praying Medic

CHAPTER ONE

Power or Authority?

A SPIRITUAL REVIVAL BROKE OUT on Azusa Street in the industrial district of Los Angeles in 1906. During the next ten years, miraculous signs and wonders were demonstrated by many of the participants. Since then, interest in spiritual power and authority has grown in communities of faith.

Many people use the terms power and authority interchangeably, but they convey two distinct ideas. While some Bible teachers do make a theoretical distinction between power and authority, few can articulate those differences in practical terms. To make matters worse, many Bible translators have confused these two words. This is particularly true of the King James Version and other translations that are based on it.

The King James is a good Bible translation; however, like all translations, when you look closely at how certain Greek and Hebrew words are translated, it becomes clear that some words could, and in many cases, *must* be translated differently.

The Greek language has a specific word for the kind of power discussed in the New Testament. The Greek word for power is *dunamis* (δύναμαι). *Strong's Concordance* gives the following definitions for this word:

1. Strength, power, ability.
2. Inherent power, power residing in a thing by virtue of its nature, or which a person or thing exerts and puts forth.
3. Power for performing miracles.
4. Moral power and excellence of soul.
5. The power and influence which belong to riches and wealth.
6. Power and resources arising from numbers.
7. Power consisting in or resting upon armies, forces, hosts.

Many of these definitions don't capture the essence of the word *dunamis* (power). Several of them sound more like definitions of authority, rather than power. Definition three (power for performing miracles) is the most accurate. *Dunamis* is best thought of as power or *energy*, like the energy that powers a mobile phone. It is kinetic energy with a divine origin—the power that created the universe, and that which Jesus and His disciples released to work miracles.

Any time the Greek word *dunamis* is found in the text of scripture, it should be translated as the English word power. Unfortunately, that is not always the case. In many places, it is translated as authority instead of power. The reverse is also true.

The Greek word for authority is *exousia* (ἐξουσία). *Strong's Concordance* defines *exousia* this way:

1. Power of choice, liberty of doing as one pleases.
2. The ability or strength with which one is endued, which he either possesses or exercises.
3. The power of authority (influence) and of right (privilege).

Note that in defining authority, it is difficult not to use the word power. The New Testament Greek word *exousia* is properly translated as authority. It is best thought of as the right of rulership. God is the ultimate ruler. His authority is limitless, matchless, and self-sustaining. He exercises authority in the heavens and delegates it to His earthly servants. Humans exercise authority in a similar way. For the remainder of this book, when you see the word authority, it will refer to the right of rulership. And when you see the word power, it will refer to energy.

Authority in Man's Kingdoms

IT WILL HELP OUR STUDY to review how authority is viewed both in the context of God's kingdom and the kingdoms of man. This chapter will examine how humans view authority.

Authority is an abstract concept until it is *exercised*. The use of authority causes a change in the realm over which it is exercised. For example, a king may exercise authority by collecting taxes or commanding that surplus food be given to the poor. However, kings often delegate authority to their servants as opposed to acting on their authority themselves. When a tax collector receives money owed in taxes, he does so under the authority granted to him by the king, as does the man who distributes bread to the poor.

A shift supervisor who works at a factory has authority over operations during his shift, which may include personnel management, scheduling, ordering supplies, and resolving employee disputes. These tasks are the way in which a supervisor exercises authority. A supervisor's authority is restricted to the hours he works and to the specific factory that employs him. He doesn't have the same authority during another supervisor's shift or at another factory. His *scope* of authority is limited, and it is also *relational*. It is granted to him, and can be revoked by the factory's manager.

The factory manager has a similar scope of authority. It is limited to the factory at which he works, and it's relational. The company's Chief Executive Officer (CEO) grants authority to his subordinates and can revoke it at his discretion. The CEO is in a similar situation; his authority is granted by the company's board of directors, whom the shareholders appoint. A CEO has the right to make major decisions involving the company's interests, but his authority can be revoked. In organizations with this type of structure, everyone in the chain of command has authority given to them by someone else. Any of them can be promoted if they exercise their authority wisely or have it removed if they exercise it poorly.

The student body president at a high school presides over the student council, facilitates council meetings, leads discussions, and advocates for the best interests of the students. She can vote on measures brought before the student council for official action. The student body grants the president authority when they elect her. In democratic organizations and societies, authority is commonly delegated to individuals through popular vote.

Citizens elect political leaders who are responsible for representing the interests of their constituents. In the United States, the Constitution gives the ultimate authority to the citizenry, who delegate their authority to elected leaders.

A student body president may one day be elected a state senator. She may also be elected to the U.S. Congress or may become President of the United States. Each position represents a different *level* of authority. Each level of authority has a different scope. While the wise use of authority may grant opportunities for advancement, the abuse of it may result in its removal by the one who granted it.

Now, let's consider a different situation: Imagine a man who claims to be the king of a country. He wears a crown and occupies a throne, but the citizens do not recognize him as their king. His decrees are ignored and his orders fall on deaf ears. Although he *claims* to have authority, it is of no effect because others do not recognize it. A man may be a rightful king, and his subjects may not recognize his authority. This peculiar situation is the subject of the next chapter.

CHAPTER THREE

Authority in God's Kingdom

THIS CHAPTER WILL EXAMINE PASSAGES from the Bible that demonstrate the nature of authority as it pertains to God's kingdom. In the parables of the New Testament, Jesus illustrated the way in which human rulers delegate authority to others. The nineteenth chapter of the book of Luke opens with Him preparing to enter Jerusalem as the Messiah. But just before He did, He spoke the following parable to His disciples:

> *Now as they heard these things, He spoke another parable, because He was near Jerusalem and because they thought the kingdom of God would appear immediately. Therefore, He said: "A certain nobleman went into a far country to receive for himself a kingdom and to return. So, he called ten of his servants, delivered to them ten minas, and said to them, 'Do business till I come.' But his citizens hated him, and sent a delegation after him, saying, 'We will not have this man to reign over us.'*

And so it was that when he returned, having received the kingdom, he then commanded these servants, to whom he had given the money, to be called to him, that he might know how much every man had gained by trading. Then came the first, saying, 'Master, your mina has earned ten minas.' And he said to him, 'Well done, good servant; because you were faithful in a very little, have authority over ten cities.' And the second came, saying, 'Master, your mina has earned five minas.' Likewise, he said to him, 'You also be over five cities.'

Then another came, saying, 'Master, here is your mina, which I have kept put away in a handkerchief. For I feared you, because you are an austere man. You collect what you did not deposit, and reap what you did not sow.' And he said to him, 'Out of your own mouth I will judge you, you wicked servant. You knew that I was an austere man, collecting what I did not deposit and reaping what I did not sow. Why then did you not put my money in the bank, that at my coming I might have collected it with interest?'

And he said to those who stood by, 'Take the mina from him, and give it to him who has ten minas.' (But they said to him, 'Master, he has ten minas.') 'For I say to you, that to everyone who has will be given; and from him who does not have, even what he has will be taken away from him. But bring here those enemies of mine, who did not want me to reign over them, and slay them before me.'"
LUKE 19:11-27

Luke's writings noted that Jesus shared this parable because His disciples thought His kingdom would appear immediately. Jesus corrected their misunderstanding. He portrayed himself as "a certain nobleman" and described His kingdom as something He would receive after traveling to a far country—an allusion to His death and resurrection. Jesus explained that He was entrusting His servants to manage His goods while He was away. He used money to represent the things He valued and said He would distribute His goods to His servants and then leave them to conduct business. He warned them that upon His return, He would make them give an account of how they had conducted business. Some would prove to be good stewards, while others would squander the opportunity.

This parable illustrates how Jesus has delegated responsibility (authority) to us in the hope that we will use it wisely. He is not physically present on the earth now. Instead, we're given the authority to represent Him and His kingdom in His absence. We are led through the operation of the Holy Spirit, who is our connection to God. When we are born again, our human spirit is empowered by God's Spirit. Once this happens, the Holy Spirit communicates with us in a variety of ways. (For more detail on this subject, check out my book *Hearing God's Voice Made Simple*.)

After giving this parable to His disciples, Jesus rode into Jerusalem on a donkey. He prophesied the city's destruction for its rebellion against God and then went into the temple and drove out those who sold animals to be used as sacrifices. Luke chapter 20 opens with the religious leaders questioning Him:

> *Now it happened on one of those days, as He taught the people in the temple and preached the gospel, that the chief priests and the scribes, together with the elders, confronted Him and spoke to Him, saying, "Tell us, by what authority are You doing these things? Or who is he who gave You this authority?"*
> LUKE 20:1-2

Jesus knew that the religious leaders would devise traps to ensnare him, hoping to find some sin of which they could falsely accuse Him. This was His response:

> *But He answered and said to them, "I also will ask you one thing, and answer Me: The baptism of John—was it from heaven or from men?"*
>
> *And they reasoned among themselves, saying, "If we say, 'From heaven,' He will say, 'Why then did you not believe him?' But if we say, 'From men,' all the people will stone us, for they are persuaded that John was a prophet." So, they answered that they did not know where it was from.*
>
> *And Jesus said to them, "Neither will I tell you by what authority I do these things."*
> LUKE 20:3-8

21

John had been authorized by God to baptize people. The religious leaders knew this, but admitting so would expose them as hypocrites, so they pretended not to know by what authority John worked. Since they refused to acknowledge the authority given to John, Jesus knew they would not recognize the authority He had received from His Father. He then spoke this parable in their presence:

> *Then He began to tell the people this parable: "A certain man planted a vineyard, leased it to vinedressers, and went into a far country for a long time. Now at vintage-time he sent a servant to the vinedressers, that they might give him some of the fruit of the vineyard. But the vinedressers beat him and sent him away empty-handed. Again, he sent another servant; and they beat him also, treated him shamefully, and sent him away empty-handed. And again, he sent a third; and they wounded him also and cast him out.*
>
> *Then the owner of the vineyard said, 'What shall I do? I will send my beloved son. Probably they will respect him when they see him.' But when the vinedressers saw him, they reasoned among themselves, saying, 'This is the heir. Come, let us kill him, that the inheritance may be ours.' So, they cast him out of the vineyard and killed him. Therefore, what will the owner of the vineyard do to them? He will come and destroy those vinedressers and give the vineyard to others."*
>
> *And when they heard it they said, "Certainly not!"*
>
> *Then He looked at them and said, "What then is this that is written:*
>   *'The stone which the builders rejected*
>   *Has become the chief cornerstone'?*
>
> *Whoever falls on that stone will be broken; but on whomever it falls, it will grind him to powder."*
>
> *And the chief priests and the scribes that very hour sought to lay hands on Him, but they feared the people—for they knew He had spoken this parable against them.*
> LUKE 20:9-19

Jesus again illustrated the kingdom of God as something that had been entrusted to His servants. God sent messengers (the prophets) to His people, the nation of Israel, but they were put to death. He then sent His Son (Jesus) who was also killed. To hammer home the point, Jesus quoted a prophecy of the Messiah as the chief cornerstone, whom the builders (the religious leaders) had rejected.

The priests and scribes knew this parable was about them. They enjoyed the pleasures that come with titles and positions that represent authority, but they were losing their followers, who were amazed at the way Jesus taught with authority. The priests and scribes wanted to kill Him but feared the reaction of the people, so they sought to take Him by deception:

So, they watched Him, and sent spies who pretended to be righteous, that they might seize on His words, in order to deliver Him to the power and the authority of the governor.

Then they asked Him, saying, "Teacher, we know that You say and teach rightly, and You do not show personal favoritism, but teach the way of God in truth: Is it lawful for us to pay taxes to Caesar or not?"

But He perceived their craftiness, and said to them, "Why do you test Me? Show Me a denarius. Whose image and inscription does it have?"

They answered and said, "Caesar's."

And He said to them, "Render therefore to Caesar the things that are Caesar's, and to God the things that are God's."

But they could not catch Him in His words in the presence of the people. And they marveled at His answer and kept silent.
LUKE 20:20-26

Jesus noted that there are earthly and heavenly rulers who exercise authority. Just as Caesar and his authorized representatives were to be obeyed, so were the representatives of God. The debate over *who* had the rightful authority to represent God was coming to a head. Matthew chapter 23 contains a scathing rebuke from Jesus to the religious leaders:

"But woe to you, scribes and Pharisees, hypocrites! For you shut up the kingdom of heaven against men; for you neither go in yourselves, nor do you allow those who are entering to go in. Woe to you, scribes and Pharisees, hypocrites! For you devour widows' houses, and for a pretense make long prayers. Therefore, you will receive greater condemnation.

Woe to you, scribes and Pharisees, hypocrites! For you travel land and sea to win one proselyte, and when he is won, you make him twice as much a son of hell as yourselves.

Woe to you, blind guides, who say, 'Whoever swears by the temple, it is nothing; but whoever swears by the gold of the temple, he is obliged to perform it.' Fools and blind! For which is greater, the gold or the temple that sanctifies the gold? And, 'Whoever swears by the altar, it is nothing; but whoever swears by the gift that is on it, he is obliged to perform it.' Fools and blind! For which is greater, the gift or the altar that sanctifies the gift? Therefore, he who swears by the altar, swears by it and by all things on it. He who swears by the temple, swears by it and by Him who dwells in it. And he who swears by heaven, swears by the throne of God and by Him who sits on it.

Woe to you, scribes and Pharisees, hypocrites! For you pay tithe of mint and anise and cummin, and have neglected the weightier matters of the law: justice and mercy and faith. These you ought to have done, without leaving the others undone. Blind guides, who strain out a gnat and swallow a camel!

Woe to you, scribes and Pharisees, hypocrites! For you cleanse the outside of the cup and dish, but inside they are full of extortion and self-indulgence. Blind Pharisee, first cleanse the inside of the cup and dish, that the outside of them may be clean also.

Woe to you, scribes and Pharisees, hypocrites! For you are like whitewashed tombs which indeed appear beautiful outwardly, but

*inside are full of dead men's bones and all uncleanness. Even so
you also outwardly appear righteous to men, but inside you are
full of hypocrisy and lawlessness.*

*Woe to you, scribes and Pharisees, hypocrites! Because you
build the tombs of the prophets and adorn the monuments of the
righteous, and say, 'If we had lived in the days of our fathers,
we would not have been partakers with them in the blood of the
prophets.'*

*Therefore, you are witnesses against yourselves that you are sons
of those who murdered the prophets. Fill up, then, the measure of
your fathers' guilt. Serpents, brood of vipers! How can you escape
the condemnation of hell? Therefore, indeed, I send you prophets,
wise men, and scribes: some of them you will kill and crucify, and
some of them you will scourge in your synagogues and persecute
from city to city, that on you may come all the righteous blood
shed on the earth, from the blood of righteous Abel to the blood of
Zechariah, son of Berechiah, whom you murdered between the
temple and the altar. Assuredly, I say to you, all these things will
come upon this generation.*

*O Jerusalem, Jerusalem, the one who kills the prophets and stones
those who are sent to her! How often I wanted to gather your children together, as a hen gathers her chicks under her wings, but
you were not willing! See! Your house is left to you desolate; for
I say to you, you shall see Me no more till you say, 'Blessed is He
who comes in the name of the Lord!'"*
MATT. 23:13-39

Jesus stated in clear and condemning terms what he thought of the
religious leaders and their claim to authority. Because they had been
publicly exposed, the scribes, priests, and Pharisees plotted to kill
Jesus. Luke chapter 22 closes with a discussion about His claim to be
the Son of God:

*As soon as it was day, the elders of the people, both chief priests
and scribes, came together and led Him into their council, saying,
"If You are the Christ, tell us."*

But He said to them, "If I tell you, you will by no means believe. And if I also ask you, you will by no means answer Me or let Me go. Hereafter the Son of Man will sit on the right hand of the power of God."

Then they all said, "Are You then the Son of God?"

So, He said to them, "You rightly say that I am."

And they said, "What further testimony do we need? For we have heard it ourselves from His own mouth."
LUKE 22:66-71

Like Jesus, the scribes and Pharisees claimed that God was their father. The implication was that people should heed their instruction because they had God's stamp of approval. The discussion continued:

They answered and said to Him, "Abraham is our father." Jesus said to them, "If you are Abraham's children, do the deeds of Abraham. But as it is, you are seeking to kill Me, a man who has told you the truth, which I heard from God; this Abraham did not do. You are doing the deeds of your father." They said to Him, "We were not born as a result of sexual immorality; we have one Father: God." Jesus said to them, "If God were your Father, you would love Me, for I came forth from God and am here; for I have not even come on My own, but He sent Me. Why do you not understand what I am saying? It is because you cannot listen to My word. You are of your father the devil, and you want to do the desires of your father. He was a murderer from the beginning, and does not stand in the truth because there is no truth in him. Whenever he tells a lie, he speaks from his own nature, because he is a liar and the father of lies."
JOHN 8:39-44 NASB

The religious leaders accused Jesus of blasphemy before Pontius Pilate because He made himself equal with God. John chapter 19 contains the discussion between Pilate and Jesus that led to his crucifixion:

So, then Pilate took Jesus and scourged Him. And the soldiers twisted a crown of thorns and put it on His head, and they put on Him a purple robe. Then they said, "Hail, King of the Jews!" And they struck Him with their hands.

Pilate then went out again, and said to them, "Behold, I am bringing Him out to you, that you may know that I find no fault in Him."

Then Jesus came out, wearing the crown of thorns and the purple robe. And Pilate said to them, "Behold the Man!"

Therefore, when the chief priests and officers saw Him, they cried out, saying, "Crucify Him, crucify Him!"

Pilate said to them, "You take Him and crucify Him, for I find no fault in Him."

The Jews answered him, "We have a law, and according to our law He ought to die, because He made Himself the Son of God."

Therefore, when Pilate heard that saying, he was the more afraid, and went again into the Praetorium, and said to Jesus, "Where are You from?" But Jesus gave him no answer.

Then Pilate said to Him, "Are You not speaking to me? Do You not know that I have power to crucify You, and power to release You?"

Jesus answered, "You could have no power at all against Me unless it had been given you from above. Therefore, the one who delivered Me to you has the greater sin."

From then on Pilate sought to release Him, but the Jews cried out, saying, "If you let this Man go, you are not Caesar's friend. Whoever makes himself a king speaks against Caesar."

When Pilate therefore heard that saying, he brought Jesus out and sat down in the judgment seat in a place that is called The Pavement, but in Hebrew, Gabbatha. Now it was the Preparation Day of the Passover, and about the sixth hour. And he said to the Jews, "Behold your King!"

But they cried out, "Away with Him, away with Him! Crucify Him!"

Pilate said to them, "Shall I crucify your King?"

The chief priests answered, "We have no king but Caesar!"

Then he delivered Him to them to be crucified. Then they took Jesus and led Him away.

And He, bearing His cross, went out to a place called the Place of a Skull, which is called in Hebrew, Golgotha, where they crucified Him, and two others with Him, one on either side, and Jesus in the center. Now Pilate wrote a title and put it on the cross. And the writing was:

JESUS OF NAZARETH, THE KING OF THE JEWS.

Then many of the Jews read this title, for the place where Jesus was crucified was near the city; and it was written in Hebrew, Greek, and Latin.

Therefore, the chief priests of the Jews said to Pilate, "Do not write, 'The King of the Jews,' but, 'He said, "I am the King of the Jews."'"

Pilate answered, "What I have written, I have written."
JOHN 19:1-22

Pilate questioned Jesus but received few answers. The Lord did not deny that He was a king, and for that crime, He was sentenced to death. At one point, Pilate said he had the power to kill Him, but Jesus countered by saying he had no power but that which was given to him by heaven. (The Greek word that is translated "power" in this verse should be translated "authority." We will cover this matter in the next chapter.) Ultimately, all rulers—even earthly ones—are under the authority of God as the Apostle Paul pointed out in his letter to the church in Rome:

Let every soul be subject to the governing authorities. For there is no authority except from God, and the authorities that exist are appointed by God. Therefore, whoever resists the authority resists

the ordinance of God, and those who resist will bring judgment on themselves.
ROM. 13:1-2

This chapter and the one previous show two divergent models of authority. Earthly kingdoms view it as the right to rule over others. Jesus demonstrated authority in serving others. Authority is a multi-faceted issue. In the chapters that follow, we will explore its practical application in a variety of common situations.

CHAPTER FOUR

Who Is in Control?

THE CHRISTIAN FAITH IS COMPRISED of thousands of denominations. Each denomination has a unique set of ideas that it teaches about the nature of God. While I draw ideas and inspiration from a variety of sources, I do not adhere to the views of a particular denomination. The ideas expressed in my books, articles and podcasts are unique to me. In this chapter, I will briefly explain my understanding of how God interacts with man with respect to authority.

Some denominations teach that God exercises complete control over the lives of individuals and the destiny of the world. Authority is permission for one to control the matters of another. If God exercises total control over our personal lives and does not delegate control to us, then the discussion of authority is meaningless. The question of who controls the affairs of man must be settled if we hope to understand how power and authority work.

Many Christians have learned to say—particularly when life is difficult—that God is in control. We reflexively comfort ourselves with these words because they act as a pain-killer when life is difficult. We seldom tell ourselves God is in control when life is rosy. John Calvin proposed five theological assertions that have become the foundation for the view that God controls our affairs. These five points can be remembered by the mnemonic T.U.L.I.P.

In the TULIP mnemonic, the letter T stands for total depravity—the idea that man is dead and cannot save himself. The letter U stands for unconditional election. God has chosen to save some people for His own reasons and has rejected others, irrespective of their personal desires or choices. The letter L stands for limited atonement—Jesus did not die for all of mankind, but only those whom God has chosen to save. The letter I stands for irresistible grace. If God has chosen to save you, there is nothing you can do to negate His will. The last letter, P stands for perseverance of the saints; once God chooses you, nothing you can do will result in the loss of your salvation. The TULIP theology of Calvin teaches that God exercises complete control over man's eternal destiny. In this arrangement, man's free will is either meaningless or non-existent. The assertions found in the TULIP mnemonic originally applied to the issue of salvation. However, over time, the idea grew into the belief that God exerts control over all of our affairs, even down to the smallest detail.

I do not question that the Bible, in certain places, teaches some of these concepts. My concern is that this view only presents one side of the issue—God's side. While it may be true from God's perspective that He has chosen some to be saved and not others, we cannot live as if He will sovereignly save anyone aside from our efforts. I am not omniscient; I don't know who has been chosen for salvation. Salvation comes by sharing the news that God loves us. From my perspective, I must exercise my free will and share God's love with others—even those who have not been chosen for salvation. A man who has no relationship with God doesn't know if he has been chosen for salvation, and neither do I.

I don't reject TULIP theology because it is untrue. I reject it because it is impossible to live by its principles in a practical way. A theology that asserts that God is in complete control leads to the negation of free will. I can't pretend that God will pick out what shirt I'll wear, decide what emails I'll respond to, or choose what I'll make for dinner. He isn't going to sovereignly drive my vehicle into the shop for an oil change. I am responsible for doing these things, and I must live with the consequences of my decisions. We cannot assert that God is in control of our lives and also believe in free will.

One can reject the theology of determinism—the doctrine that everything is determined by God—without rejecting the notion that God is active in our lives. Our Creator attempts to influence our thoughts and actions by communicating with us through the ministry of the Holy Spirit. Influence, however, is not control. We are responsible for hearing God's voice. And we have the freedom to heed or ignore His promptings. God is always speaking to us, bidding us to do His will as His representatives, but He does not exert control over our will.

The idea that God is in control is pleasing as an abstract concept, but it cannot be applied in everyday life. I can't live as if God controls my personal decisions. I must live as if I have free will, and the exercise of it has real and lasting consequences. If free will is a personal reality, it must be applied to all of society. And when it is, the depraved forces at work in our world come into view. One needs only to scan the day's news headlines to understand that sinful, selfish humans influenced by evil are, in fact, in control of the worst events playing out on our planet.

We interact with God not as automatons but as intelligent beings with the capacity to choose. The way we view our Creator determines the kind of relationship we will have with Him. We may choose to see Him as a friend or foe. He respects our decisions, and our choices define the terms of the relationship. If we see Him as a friend, we open the door to partnering with Him. When we partner with Him, He grants us power and authority.

CHAPTER FIVE

How Does Authority Work?

GOD IS THE SOURCE OF all authority in the universe. He could retain personal authority—or control, if you prefer—over the affairs of His creation. Instead, He has chosen to delegate a measure of authority to those He created. The psalmist noted that although God controls the affairs of heaven, He has chosen not to do so with the affairs of mankind:

> *The heaven, even the heavens, are the Lord's; But the earth He has given to the children of men.*
> PSALMS 115:16

Delegated authority is permission granted to one person to represent the interests of another. The one who gives authority to another does so because they prefer not to manage their affairs personally. This arrangement makes authority dependent upon a relationship. One grants authority, while the other exercises it.

The authority that one receives from another usually gives the freedom to make decisions without requiring special permission before it is exercised. Permission is granted to act on behalf of another independently. The exercise of authority is generally at the discretion of the one to whom it is granted, even if its use is not wise or beneficial to the one granting it. The one who has been given authority has the freedom to make both good and bad decisions. For example, if I allow my son to use my car, he has permission to go wherever he wants, and with whomever he wants. While I may not approve of his choices, he has the freedom to do as he pleases. Generally, the wise exercise of authority provides an opportunity for promotion to a higher level of authority, while poor exercise leads to a reduction or complete removal of it. An example of this principle is seen in 2 Kings chapter 1, where Elijah called down fire from heaven to consume the soldiers that had been sent to him:

Then the king sent to him a captain of fifty with his fifty men. So, he went up to him; and there he was, sitting on the top of a hill. And he spoke to him: "Man of God, the king has said, 'Come down!'"

So, Elijah answered and said to the captain of fifty, "If I am a man of God, then let fire come down from heaven and consume you and your fifty men." And fire came down from heaven and consumed him and his fifty. Then he sent to him another captain of fifty with his fifty men.

And he answered and said to him: "Man of God, thus has the king said, 'Come down quickly!'"

So, Elijah answered and said to them, "If I am a man of God, let fire come down from heaven and consume you and your fifty men." And the fire of God came down from heaven and consumed him and his fifty.

Again, he sent a third captain of fifty with his fifty men. And the third captain of fifty went up, and came and fell on his knees before Elijah, and pleaded with him, and said to him: "Man of God, please let my life and the life of these fifty servants of yours be precious in your sight. Look, fire has come down from heaven and burned up the first two captains of fifties with their fifties. But let my life now be precious in your sight."

And the angel of the Lord said to Elijah, "Go down with him; do not be afraid of him." So, he arose and went down with him to the king.
2 KINGS 1:2-17

God granted Elijah the authority to call down fire from heaven. This authority was not limited only to cases that were approved by God. When Elijah unwisely exercised his authority, the Lord did not negate it but sent an angel to correct him.

Disciples of Jesus are given a multitude of types and levels of authority. As God's representatives, our authority encompasses many areas. But unlike in the kingdoms of man, where one person is given authority over another, we are not given such authority. The believer is subject only to the authority of Christ. We do not have other humans in authority over us, and we have no authority over others. While we may have teachers and people who encourage and train us, these individuals do not exercise authority over us.

Throughout history, governments and military institutions have exercised authority over individuals. Jesus said this model would not be allowed among His disciples. When a woman asked Him to give her sons positions of authority in His kingdom, He explained that His kingdom employs a different model of authority:

Then the mother of Zebedee's sons came to Him with her sons, kneeling down and asking something from Him.

And He said to her, "What do you wish?"

She said to Him, "Grant that these two sons of mine may sit, one on Your right hand and the other on the left, in Your kingdom."

But Jesus answered and said, "You do not know what you ask. Are you able to drink the cup that I am about to drink, and be baptized with the baptism that I am baptized with?"

They said to Him, "We are able."

So, He said to them, "You will indeed drink My cup, and be baptized with the baptism that I am baptized with; but to sit on My right hand and on My left is not Mine to give, but it is for those for whom it is prepared by My Father."

And when the ten heard it, they were greatly displeased with the two brothers. But Jesus called them to Himself and said, "You know that the rulers of the Gentiles lord it over them, and those who are great exercise authority over them. Yet it shall not be so among you; but whoever desires to become great among you, let him be your servant. And whoever desires to be first among you, let him be your slave—just as the Son of Man did not come to be served, but to serve, and to give His life a ransom for many."
MATT. 20:20-28

In the kingdoms of man, authority is the right to be served by others. Authority in God's kingdom is attained by serving others in humility —a principle Jesus demonstrated. The authority we receive from God allows us to defeat sickness and disease, cast out demons, and calm storms. We may be given the authority to speak on certain subjects. Some are given authority to influence the communities of music and art. Others are given authority to influence the fields of physics and chemistry, while still others have the authority to represent God's interests in the field of medicine. These are just a few examples of the areas of society God grants us authority in which to operate. As we identify the areas of authority He has given us, and as we represent His interests in accordance with His desires, our level or sphere of authority may change.

Our relationship with God is the key to our authority. We begin by asking Him to reveal the areas over which we've been given authority. That requires us to develop the ability to communicate with Him. Next, we must learn *how* He wants us to exercise authority in those areas. Again, this requires the ability to hear His voice. As our relationship grows, we'll receive more details about how He wants us to exercise authority.

CHAPTER SIX

Sovereign Miracle or Human Obedience?

THE BIBLE IS FILLED WITH stories that describe incredible miracles. Religious leaders often relate these stories as sovereign acts of God— events that required no human participation. However, if a miracle involved man's cooperation, it suggests that God granted some authority to the individual. In this chapter, we'll survey a few of these stories to determine if they were sovereign acts of God or if they involved man's cooperation.

When the Israelites fled Egypt, God instructed Moses to lead His people toward the Red Sea. This move was counterintuitive. It left no way of escape from the army of Pharaoh that pursued them. But God had a plan, and it required the cooperation of Moses. The Lord was going to make a way for the Israelites to pass through the Red Sea on dry ground. However, rather than parting the sea Himself, God instructed Moses to do it:

Then the Lord said to Moses, "Why are you crying out to Me? Tell the sons of Israel to go forward. As for you, lift up your staff and reach out with your hand over the sea and divide it, and the sons of Israel shall go through the midst of the sea on dry land.
EX. 14:15-16 NASB

Moses asked God to rescue the Israelites. The Lord told Moses it was his responsibility and explained what he needed to do. When he obeyed the instructions and raised his staff, the sea parted, and the Israelites went to the opposite shore on dry ground.

It may seem obvious, but I would like to point out that the sea did not part *until* Moses obeyed God's instruction and stretched out his staff. Moses exercised the authority God had given him. His staff represented that authority. Believing God's promise that the sea would part, *by faith*, he raised his staff (his symbol of authority), and the waters parted. We can logically infer that had Moses *not* believed God's promise, he would *not* have raised his staff, and the sea would *not* have parted. The parting of the Red Sea, which is often attributed solely to God, was, in fact, a collaborative effort. It required the cooperation of a man who exercised his God-given authority.

The Israelites wandered for years in the wilderness rather than enter the promised land. When they finally agreed to accept God's promise, the Lord said they would cross the Jordan River on dry ground. But once again, the parting of the water would require faith and obedience on the part of man.

And it shall come to pass, as soon as the soles of the feet of the priests who bear the ark of the Lord, the Lord of all the earth, shall rest in the waters of the Jordan, that the waters of the Jordan shall be cut off, the waters that come down from upstream, and they shall stand as a heap."

So it was, when the people set out from their camp to cross over the Jordan, with the priests bearing the ark of the covenant before the people, and as those who bore the ark came to the Jordan, and the feet of the priests who bore the ark dipped in the edge of the water (for the Jordan overflows all its banks during the whole

time of harvest), that the waters which came down from upstream stood still, and rose in a heap very far away at Adam, the city that is beside Zaretan. So, the waters that went down into the Sea of the Arabah, the Salt Sea, failed, and were cut off; and the people crossed over opposite Jericho. Then the priests who bore the ark of the covenant of the Lord stood firm on dry ground in the midst of the Jordan; and all Israel crossed over on dry ground, until all the people had crossed completely over the Jordan.
JOSH. 3:13-17

In the same way that the Red Sea did not part until Moses raised his staff, the waters of the Jordan did not give way until the priests stood in the river. The priests *believed* God's promise and, in obedience, did as He commanded. Had they *not* believed and *not* obeyed, the waters of the Jordan would *not* have parted. The miracle was not a sovereign act of God—it required participation by man.

Let's look at an example that illustrates the ministry of healing taught to Moses. Because the Israelites lived in the desert wilderness, they were sometimes bitten by poisonous snakes. So, God proposed a solution:

Then the Lord said to Moses, "Make a fiery serpent, and set it on a pole; and it shall be that everyone who is bitten, when he looks at it, shall live." So, Moses made a bronze serpent, and put it on a pole; and so it was, if a serpent had bitten anyone, when he looked at the bronze serpent, he lived.
NUM. 21:8-9

The serpent on the pole foreshadowed the crucifixion of Jesus:

And as Moses lifted up the serpent in the wilderness, even so must the Son of Man be lifted up, that whoever believes in Him should not perish but have eternal life.
JOHN 3:14-15

God instructed Moses that anyone bitten by a snake should look at the bronze serpent on the pole, and they would be healed. The bite of a serpent portrays, metaphorically, how sin affects us. A venomous snake bite can be lethal. Similarly, the consequence of sin is death. But God offers forgiveness of sin to those who will receive it. He also provided physical healing of a snake bite to those who gazed upon the serpent on the pole. We can infer that if someone chose *not* to look at the serpent, they would *not* be healed and would likely die of the snake's bite.

Then, as now, God offers healing to those who are willing to receive it, but healing requires faith. One must believe in God's promise. If a healer is involved, that individual must believe in God's promise of healing. If one is not involved, the one who needs healing must believe they will be healed and (in some cases) take action based on that belief. If an Israelite believed he *could* be healed but never looked at the serpent on the pole, they would be in disobedience to God's command and could not expect to be healed. For the healing to occur, they had to both believe God *and* put that faith into action by gazing upon the serpent. Although God does occasionally work sovereign miracles, many times, our cooperation is required.

CHAPTER SEVEN

Authority for Healing

MANY OF US HAVE BEEN taught that miracles of healing happen when we ask God to heal someone who is sick or injured. We pray, and God hears our prayer. Then, based on His knowledge of the situation, He decides to either heal the individual or leave them as they are. I won't say that God never answers such prayers. But after trying this approach with hundreds of my patients and seeing none of them healed, I asked the Lord repeatedly, "What am I missing? Show me what I need to know." In time, I discovered a better, more biblical approach. A handful of verses from the gospels of Luke and Matthew shed light on how divine healing is intended to work.

The sixth, seventh, and eighth chapters of the gospel of Luke record how Jesus healed the sick and infirmed, delivered others from demons, and raised two people from the dead. Jesus chose twelve disciples and empowered them to do the same:

*Then He called His twelve disciples together and gave them power
and authority over all demons, and to cure diseases. He sent them
to preach the kingdom of God and to heal the sick.*
LUKE 9:1-2

Jesus gave His disciples two things: power and authority. He did so to
accomplish two purposes: Healing diseases and removing demons. The
parallel passage in Matthew chapter 10 provides more details:

*"And as you go, preach, saying, 'The kingdom of heaven is at hand.'
Heal the sick, cleanse the lepers, raise the dead, cast out demons."*
MATT. 10:7-8

The disciples were told to raise the dead, cast out demons, and heal
incurable diseases. In Luke chapter 10, we read how Jesus commissioned
seventy of His disciples. Here's verse one from that chapter:

*After these things the Lord appointed seventy others also, and sent
them two by two before His face into every city and place where
He Himself was about to go.*

Verses eight and nine of this chapter contain His healing instruction:

*Whatever city you enter, and they receive you, eat such things as
are set before you. And heal the sick there, and say to them, 'The
kingdom of God has come near to you.'*
LUKE 10:8-9

Jesus didn't tell His disciples to *ask God* for healing. Instead, he *gave
them* power and authority and instructed *them* to heal the sick, work
miracles, and declare the kingdom of God has come. Although the
power and authority needed to cast out demons and heal the sick come
from God, it is wielded by us, His representatives. An example of the
use of authority for healing is found in Matthew chapter eight, where
Jesus healed the Roman Centurion's servant:

*Now when Jesus had entered Capernaum, a centurion came to
Him, pleading with Him, saying, "Lord, my servant is lying at
home paralyzed, dreadfully tormented."*

And Jesus said to him, "I will come and heal him."

The Centurion answered and said, "Lord, I am not worthy that You should come under my roof. But only speak a word, and my servant will be healed. For I also am a man under authority, having soldiers under me. And I say to this one, 'Go,' and he goes; and to another, 'Come,' and he comes; and to my servant, 'Do this,' and he does it."

When Jesus heard it, He marveled, and said to those who followed, "Assuredly, I say to you, I have not found such great faith, not even in Israel!"

... Jesus said to the Centurion, "Go your way; and as you have believed, so let it be done for you." And his servant was healed that same hour.
MATT. 8:5-10, 13

The Centurion recognized the authority Jesus had over sickness. Because he understood how authority works, his faith apprehended healing for his servant. No prayer was involved; Jesus spoke a word, and the servant was healed. It was a simple transaction involving the faith of the Centurion and the authority of Jesus. The servant was healed *by* the authority of Jesus *through* the Centurion's faith. (The dynamics of faith will be discussed in another chapter.)

A couple of points are worth considering: First, when authority is exercised for healing, distance is not an issue. Jesus was not in direct contact with the Centurion's servant. Authority is exercised independently of proximity. I pray for people who live thousands of miles away, and they're healed after I make a command or declaration. Second, Jesus did not ask for the name of the Centurion's servant. This information is not needed to exercise authority. In many cases, when I pray for someone, I don't know their name or what illness they have. Another example of the exercise of authority is found in Matthew chapter nine:

Getting into a boat, Jesus crossed over the Sea of Galilee and came to His own city. And they brought to Him a paralyzed man lying on a stretcher. And seeing their faith, Jesus said to the man who

45

was paralyzed, "Take courage, son; your sins are forgiven." And some of the scribes said to themselves, "This man is blaspheming!" And Jesus, perceiving their thoughts, said, "Why are you think-ing evil in your hearts? For which is easier, to say, 'Your sins are forgiven,' or to say, 'Get up and walk'? But so that you may know that the Son of Man has authority on earth to forgive sins"—then He said to the paralyzed man, "Get up, pick up your stretcher and go home." And he got up and went home. But when the crowds saw this, they were awestruck, and they glorified God, who had given such authority to men.

MATT. 9:1-8

This passage provides a wealth of information about the way in which authority is exercised for healing. Note how Matthew highlighted the fact that Jesus *saw the faith* of the paralytic's friends. The Lord was pleased that the lame man's friends had faith (confidence) that he would be healed.

Jesus didn't need to confront the scribes to heal the paralytic, but doing so allowed Him to demonstrate the scope of His authority. He told the paralytic his sins were forgiven. The scribes correctly observed that only God can forgive sins. In doing so, Jesus made himself equal with God. Anyone can claim to be equal with God, but such a claim would need evidence before it would be believed. To prove that His claim was true, Jesus planned to heal the paralytic. However, he did not touch the lame man. Doing so would have released power, and the Lord wanted to demonstrate His *authority*. Instead, he told the man to stand up, pick up his bed and walk home. By faith, the man did exactly that. Even though he was paralyzed, he attempted to rise under his own power. He tried to stand because he believed (he was confident) that Jesus had the authority to heal him. When he attempted to stand, his body was healed. His faith appropriated his healing. The healing testified to the fact that Jesus has the authority to forgive sins. A similar account is found in the third chapter of the book of Acts:

Now Peter and John went up together to the temple at the hour of prayer, the ninth hour. And a certain man lame from his mother's womb was carried, whom they laid daily at the gate of the temple which is called Beautiful, to ask alms from those who entered the

temple; who, seeing Peter and John about to go into the temple, asked for alms. And fixing his eyes on him, with John, Peter said, "Look at us." So, he gave them his attention, expecting to receive something from them. Then Peter said, "Silver and gold I do not have, but what I do have I give you: In the name of Jesus Christ of Nazareth, rise up and walk." And he took him by the right hand and lifted him up, and immediately his feet and ankle bones received strength. So, he, leaping up, stood and walked and entered the temple with them—walking, leaping, and praising God. And all the people saw him walking and praising God.
ACTS 3:1-9

Once again, we see faith in operation. Peter told the lame man to stand up. To do so, he would need to be healed. He believed Peter had the authority to heal him, so he tried to obey the command. As he attempted to stand, his body was healed.

I have many friends who operate in healing. Occasionally, one will encounter someone who uses a wheelchair because they cannot walk. First, the friend will share a few testimonies of healing. Then, when the one in the wheelchair asks if they can be healed, my friend will tell them to get out of the wheelchair. In some cases, as they try to stand, they'll suddenly realize their affliction has been healed, and they no longer need the wheelchair.

Luke chapter 17 provides another glimpse of how authority brings healing:

Now it happened as He went to Jerusalem that He passed through the midst of Samaria and Galilee. Then as He entered a certain village, there met Him ten men who were lepers, who stood afar off. And they lifted up their voices and said, "Jesus, Master, have mercy on us!"

So, when He saw them, He said to them, "Go, show yourselves to the priests." And so it was that as they went, they were cleansed.

And one of them, when he saw that he was healed, returned, and with a loud voice glorified God, and fell down on his face at His feet, giving Him thanks. And he was a Samaritan.

So, Jesus answered and said, "Were there not ten cleansed? But where are the nine? Were there not any found who returned to give glory to God except this foreigner?" And He said to him, "Arise, go your way. Your faith has made you well."
LUKE 17:11-19

Note how the lepers asked Jesus to show mercy upon them. They knew He had the authority to heal them, and they wanted to be made well. As in the previous examples where authority was exercised, Jesus gave a command to those who needed healing. If an individual believed they could be healed, they would obey the command. Their faith (demonstrated by their obedience) appropriated their healing.

The exercise of authority in the realm of healing usually involves issuing a command of some kind. There are many ways this can be done. It does not necessarily require a command to be given to the one who needs healing. When Jesus healed the Centurion's servant, he did not command the servant to do anything. He spoke a word, and the servant was healed. We might infer that the Lord commanded a demon to leave or that he rebuked a disease.

There are three components to healing by the exercise of authority: A command is given, and when faith is present, the body obeys the command and is healed. The one with faith could be the person who needs healing, or it may be a friend or relative. In most cases, however, the one issuing the command is expected to have faith that the body will respond to the exercise of authority.

In most cases, I command damaged or diseased parts of the body to be healed. As a general approach to healing injured joints (the wrist, elbow, shoulder, knee, or ankle), I'll command all bones, nerves, ligaments, tendons, muscles, and cartilage to be healed. With the knee, I'll add the meniscus to the above list. With the shoulder, I'll add the rotator cuff to the above list. If the person suffered a traumatic injury, I'll add blood vessels and soft tissues to the list. If the person knows that a particular part of the body is diseased or injured, I'll focus on that part of the body. I'll make the commands, and then, if the person is with me, I'll ask if they feel any changes. I'll ask them to test the range of motion for the injured joint and rate the pain on a scale from one to ten. If their range of motion is not yet normal, or if pain is still present, I'll repeat the process until the pain is gone and their range of motion is normal.

With injuries of the spine, I'll typically command discs, nerves, muscles, ligaments, bones, and the spinal cord to be healed. Then, I'll ask the individual to check their range of motion and evaluate their pain. I continue the process until they're pain-free and have normal range of motion and sensation.

Physiologically speaking, I expect the injured or diseased tissues of the body to obey my command. All of creation is subject to the authority of God, and as His authorized representatives, creation obeys our commands too. The body creates a new disc in the spine, a new meniscus in the knee, a new rotator cuff in the shoulder, new nerves in the feet, or a new kidney. Whatever is needed to obey the command, the body creates it. If the skin needs healing, I command it to be made new. Conditions affecting the eyes and ears can be approached in a similar fashion. You can command the eyes or ears to be made new. An alternate approach is speaking to the eye and instructing it to see normally. If you know a particular structure of the eye or ear is diseased, such as the macula, retina, or cochlea, focus on that structure and command it to be made new.

Next, I'll share a testimony that illustrates this principle.

One day, while working as a paramedic, I transported an elderly woman who came down with the flu. I informed her that there wasn't anything the hospital could do for her and that she might be better off staying home. However, she insisted on going to a hospital, so we prepared to transport her. While loading her in the ambulance, I obtained her medical history. She was generally healthy except for severe scoliosis, arthritis, and a torn meniscus in her left knee. The torn meniscus got my attention.

About a month earlier, I prayed for a young woman at a grocery store who had the same condition. I saw her in a wheelchair leaving the store and asked if I could pray for her. After a few minutes of prayer, she was healed. Having done it before, I believed this woman would be healed too. So, I told her about the healing at the grocery store. "Would you like me to pray with you to be healed?"

"That would be wonderful!" She replied.

She had limited range of motion in her left knee, with severe pain when she flexed the joint. I told her to relax and placed my hand on her knee. "I command this knee to be healed in Jesus' name. I command spirits of pain to leave. What do you feel?"

"Wow, that's strange. It feels very warm."

I didn't have to ask her to flex it. She did, and her mouth dropped open.

"How did you do that?" She had full range of motion with no pain in her knee. She grabbed my hands. "Thank you. Thank you so much!"

After a short celebration in the ambulance, I asked about her back. "You have scoliosis. Does it cause pain?"

"I do have pain, but I've grown used to it. I used to be four inches taller than I am now."

"Can I pray for your back to be healed?"

"Of course, you can!"

I placed my hand on her back and commanded it to be healed. She felt heat in her spine. Her pain was gone before we arrived at the hospital.

Now, let's look at a different application of authority. When a disease process involves the presence of something that should not be there, one approach is to command it to leave. Bacterial, viral, yeast, and parasite infections are examples of invading organisms that can be commanded to leave. Tumors may also be commanded to leave. The tissues of the body are expected to obey the command when it is made in faith. An alternate approach is to speak death to the invading organism. This approach is highly effective with conditions like Lyme disease and cancer.

Although I do not recommend relying on formulas, I've found that, more often than not, God will lead me to use one tactic more than any other for healing cancer. The approach itself is not complicated; it's probably the simplest of all the methods I use. However, understanding the principle behind it requires an examination of the method Jesus used when exercising authority for healing.

As noted previously, Jesus made a command that could not be obeyed unless the body of the individual was healed. Let's look at one more example of this principle:

> *And He entered the synagogue again, and a man was there who had a withered hand. So, they watched Him closely, whether He would heal him on the Sabbath, so that they might accuse Him. And He said to the man who had the withered hand, "Step forward." Then He said to them, "Is it lawful on the Sabbath to do good or to do evil, to save life or to kill?" But they kept silent. And when He had looked around at them with anger, being grieved by the hardness of their hearts, He said to the man, "Stretch out your hand." And he stretched it out, and his hand was restored as whole as the other.*
> MARK 3:1-5

Jesus told the man to stretch out his withered hand. He would not be able to do so unless the hand was first healed. By faith, the man tried to obey the Lord's command. As he did, the muscles, nerves, ligaments, tendons, and bones were healed. The key in this case (and similar ones) is that a command was given, which would be impossible to obey unless the body was first healed.

If you want to exercise authority this way, you might say to a paralytic, "Stand up and walk," as Jesus did for one man. For the paralyzed person to obey your command, their body must be healed. If, in faith, they rise up, their body will be healed so that your command is obeyed.

The same principle can be used to heal other diseases. For example, you might hand a book to a person who is blind and tell them to read it. If they're going to read it, their eyes must first be healed. If the person has faith and they try to read the book, their sight may be restored.

51

In summary: A command or decree is issued. If it is to be followed, the body must be healed. If the individual believes they can be healed, they will take action. When the action is taken, they are healed. Next, I'll share a couple of examples of how I use this principle.

I received two prayer requests two days in a row for the healing of tumors. One request was for a woman who had a thyroid tumor. She was going to have a biopsy the following day. I closed my eyes, and, in my mind, I saw a throne. Having never seen anything like this before, I assumed it was a direction from the Holy Spirit to exercise authority as a ruler might. Rather than command the tumor to die or rebuke an evil spirit as I normally would, I made the following decree: "When the doctors take this woman into the operating room, they will not find the tumor." That was all I said. For this decree to come to pass, the tumor would need to disappear. I received a message the following day reporting precisely that. The hospital staff took the woman into the suite to do the biopsy, and the tumor, which was clearly visible on the medical images, had mysteriously vanished.

The next day, I received a request to pray for someone with a brain tumor. This person was scheduled for surgery the following day. Once again, when I closed my eyes, I saw a throne. Realizing it was a suggestion from God to use this approach again, I made the following declaration: "When they take the patient into the operating room, they will not find the tumor." I did not say anything else. I received a message the following day saying the surgeon did everything as he normally would to remove the tumor, but when the skull was opened, it could not be found. The tumor had mysteriously disappeared.

Since then, I've received many more testimonies of cancer healing. When the Holy Spirit shows me a throne, this is how I address the situation. I make a decree such that the body must be healed if it is to be obeyed. I would encourage readers not to create a healing formula from these examples. Instead, consider these stories I've shared as illustrations of general principles.

Authority can be exercised in a variety of ways. Sometimes we'll command structures of the body to be healed. Other times, we'll tell the sick person to take an action in faith. And in still other cases, we can issue an authoritative declaration of the outcome. What is the best way to heal a particular condition? Let me explain how I make that decision.

A symptom such as knee pain can have a variety of causes. It could be caused by a physiologic injury. It could be the result of an emotional wound, or it may be caused by a spirit of pain. The best approach is the one that addresses the root cause. Healing knee pain may require a release of power to create a new meniscus, the exercise of authority to remove a demon, or the healing of an emotional wound. It's impossible to know in advance which approach will be needed. For that reason, I can't say what is the best approach for healing a particular condition. The best approach is to ask God to reveal the root cause of the problem and then reveal the solution. Those who struggle with healing would be more successful if they learned to hear God more clearly and asked for specific directions.

If you're not certain you hear God accurately, you can use a process of elimination. First, command the body's physical structures to be healed and then command spirits of pain to leave. If the condition is healed, no further action is needed. But if the condition persists, and especially if the symptoms resolve initially and then return, emotional healing and deliverance are indicated, or it may require a release of power. Those subjects are addressed in the chapters that follow.

Exercise

Find someone who needs healing of a joint injury. Ask if you can pray for them to be healed. Check their level of pain and range of motion. Command the injured body part to be healed. Recheck the person's level of pain and range of motion. If the severity of pain is decreased and range of motion is improved, but the joint is not completely healed, continue commanding the body part(s) to be healed and recheck their range of motion and pain severity.

CHAPTER EIGHT

Authority Over Demons

THE AUTHORITY WE RECEIVE FROM Jesus has a variety of applications. It can be used to cure diseases, and it is the mechanism by which evil spirits (demons) are removed. Most Bible translations refer to the removal of a demon as an evil spirit being *cast out*. Some cultures call this *exorcism*. Others refer to it as *deliverance*. All these terms refer to the same process.

Let's look at an example of this from Acts chapter 16:

> *Now it happened, as we went to prayer, that a certain slave girl possessed with a spirit of divination met us, who brought her masters much profit by fortune-telling. This girl followed Paul and us, and cried out, saying, "These men are the servants of the Most High God, who proclaim to us the way of salvation." And this she did for many days. But Paul, greatly annoyed, turned and said*

to the spirit, "I command you in the name of Jesus Christ to come out of her." And he came out that very hour.
ACTS 16:16-18

Demons are disembodied spirits. They don't have physical bodies, as we do, but spiritual ones. But they desire to interact in both the spiritual and physical worlds. Because they have no physical bodies, their ability to interact in the physical world is limited. Thus, a demon must attach itself to a physical body. Once it does, it exerts influence over its host to accomplish its agenda.

There is some confusion about the way demons affect humans. Many Bible translations use the word *possession* to describe the way demons influence us. A better translation is the word *demonized*. Demonization is a matter of influence rather than complete control of the individual. Demonization occurs on a spectrum from minor to severe. One person may be only slightly affected by the presence of a demon and only in one area of life, such as addiction or lust. These people do not show outward signs of demonization. Others are severely affected.

Evil spirits can influence an individual in multiple areas of life, and they may be influenced by many demons simultaneously. Some demons inflict symptoms of chronic pain that mimic an injury. Many times there will be no other signs of demonization in someone who is harassed by a spirit of pain.

Over a span of two years, my EMT partner was healed of headaches, neck pain, back pain, knee pain, and a nasty injury to his hand. One day, he complained of knee pain that was bad enough to make him limp. I commanded his knee to be healed, as I had done many times before, but nothing happened. After five attempts, the pain was still present. That surprised me since knee pain usually responds quickly to this approach. Then it dawned on me that I had not commanded the spirit of pain to leave.

When I ask the Holy Spirit to show me details about a person's condition, He frequently shows me a demon of some kind. Because I had seen them so often, I developed a habit of commanding spirits of pain and sickness to leave. But this time, I didn't, and my partner's knee was not healed. So, I commanded the spirit of pain to leave. Next, I commanded his knee to be healed. He felt heat in his knee, and in a few minutes, it was healed.

If a condition does not improve by commanding injured body parts to be healed, you should command evil spirits to leave, even if their presence is not discerned. If the person suddenly experiences pain they didn't have before, or if a present sensation of pain moves to another part of the body or becomes worse, it's a sure sign that an evil spirit is at work. Command the demon to leave. The command need not be made in a dramatic fashion. I've done this in hospital settings where such displays are frowned upon. I command demons to leave in a low tone of voice. Sometimes, I issue the command in my mind, silently.

You may be wondering why pain would worsen during prayer. When pain increases or moves to another part of the body during prayer, a demon is trying to create fear in the mind of the afflicted individual, so they will ask us to stop praying with them, thinking that we're making things worse. When this happens, tell the person a spirit is present, and the increased pain is a tactic being used to frighten them. Then, ask if you may continue and reassure them the pain will eventually leave.

One evening, I was praying for my wife to be healed of neck pain, which was so severe it left her in tears at bedtime. I'd been praying with her for months, to no avail. That night, I did something foolish. In desperation, I asked God to put her afflictions on me if it would take away her pain. I went to sleep and had a dream where I looked for something I couldn't find. This is a classic dream God gives to people who are searching for answers.

A few seconds after waking from the dream, I felt something like a net being spread over me. Then, I realized I couldn't move my arms or legs. I could only roll from side to side. I tried to speak, but no words came out. All I could do was mumble incomprehensibly. I knew that what had gripped me was a demon. As my voice left, I tried to say, "Get out, in the name of Jesus," but I could only mumble. My rolling back and forth woke up my wife. She immediately knew a demon had overpowered me and began praying in tongues. She then commanded the demon to leave. A few seconds later, my voice returned, and the paralysis left.

My mistake was asking God to put my wife's afflictions on me. In doing so, I permitted the kingdom of darkness to attack me, and the demon was happy to visit me. Never ask for the afflictions of someone else. Never make deals with the enemy, and never invite sickness or torment into your life.

When the presence of a demon is detected, and if the one it is afflicting gives permission to have it removed, we can command it to leave using our authority. Demons will not always leave after a single command. And even if one does, it may return. Jesus explained the dynamics of demonic oppression to His disciples. That discussion is found in Luke chapter 11:

> *And He was casting out a demon, and it was mute. So it was, when the demon had gone out, that the mute spoke; and the multitudes marveled. But some of them said, "He casts out demons by Beelzebub, the ruler of the demons."*

> *Others, testing Him, sought from Him a sign from heaven. But He, knowing their thoughts, said to them: "Every kingdom divided against itself is brought to desolation, and a house divided against a house falls. If Satan also is divided against himself, how will his kingdom stand? Because you say I cast out demons by Beelzebub. And if I cast out demons by Beelzebub, by whom do your sons cast them out? Therefore, they will be your judges. But if I cast out demons with the finger of God, surely the kingdom of God has come upon you.*
> LUKE 11:14-20

Jesus explained that it was foolish to think one could cast out the servants of Satan (demons) by the authority of Satan. He then explained what happens when a demon returns to a person after it has been removed:

> *"When a strong man, fully armed, guards his own palace, his goods are in peace. But when a stronger than he comes upon him and overcomes him, he takes from him all his armor in which he trusted, and divides his spoils...When an unclean spirit goes out of a man, he goes through dry places, seeking rest; and finding none, he says, 'I will return to my house from which I came.' And*

when he comes, he finds it swept and put in order. Then he goes and takes with him seven other spirits more wicked than himself, and they enter and dwell."
LUKE 11:21-22, 24-26

Jesus likened an evil spirit to a strongman who is armored and keeps his home. (Note that demons see our bodies as their homes.) He went on to say that when one who is stronger comes, he removes the demon's armor, evicts him from the place he calls home, and divides his goods. The "goods" He spoke of are the areas of a person's life that are held in bondage by the demon. This typically manifests as physical illness or emotional trauma. He said that once removed, the demon may return to its home later if the dwelling remains intact.

How do we remove a demonic home?

Some teach that a person must be filled with the Holy Spirit to prevent a demon from returning. That idea isn't implied in this teaching and I know many Spirit-filled people who are attacked by demons. I believe Jesus illustrated a different dynamic.

Demons afflict us for specific reasons. The exercise of authority may remove an evil spirit and its disease, but the spirit and the affliction will return if the root cause is not addressed. In some cases, the evil spirit will bring other demons who afflict us with more diseases.

The battle against recurring illness and pain caused by demons is like the way we might deal with a criminal who repeatedly breaks into our home. Burglars are opportunistic. They size up their victims and evaluate their defenses, looking for signs of vulnerability. They look for alarm systems, unlocked doors and windows, the absence of a dog, and the likelihood that the homeowner will be unarmed. They look for homeowners that are the least likely to fight back. Demons do the same thing. They look for points of entry into our lives through anger, unforgiveness, pride, and emotional wounds.

The first step in defending ourselves is removing the things that allow the enemy to gain access to us. The second is learning to go on the offensive against these intruders when they visit us. Those who have not learned to exercise authority over the enemy are like homeowners who do not secure their homes or fight back against an intruder. As a result, they make themselves easy targets for evil spirits. Once word gets out in the demonic community that someone is an easy target, they can expect to be harassed by even more evil spirits.

Years ago, I experienced chronic neck pain that would leave when I received prayer, only to return a few days later. One day, I went to a healing conference and asked a woman to pray for me. She closed her eyes and asked if I held any anger toward anyone. She asked the Holy Spirit to show me who I was angry with and told me to release the anger and forgive them. I closed my eyes and, in my mind, saw an image of the CEO of the company where my wife worked. He had not been treating her fairly, and that caused me to be angry with him. I said, "I release my anger, and I forgive him." As soon as I said these words, the pain in my neck left and didn't return.

A couple of valuable lessons came from this experience. The first is that chronic pain can be caused by holding onto emotions like anger. The second is that pain can be removed by releasing the emotion. This is the principle the apostle Paul spoke of in this exhortation to the church in Ephesus:

> "In your anger do not sin": Do not let the sun go down while you are still angry, and do not give the devil a foothold.
> EPH. 4:26-27 NIV

Paul's statement implies that negative emotions like anger and hatred create opportunities for evil spirits to afflict us. The exercise of authority will temporarily drive an evil spirit away. When a demon leaves, so does the pain. But if the demon's home has not been removed—if the negative emotion and the trauma that caused it are still present—the spirit will return, and along with it, so will the pain.

The anger I was holding served as a foothold for a spirit of pain. When someone prayed with me for healing, the spirit would leave, only to return because it still had a home in my soul, created by anger. The solution came when I realized that even though I didn't value this person very highly, God did. That truth caused a change of heart.

I realized I had no right to be angry, so I forgave him and released the anger. Releasing my anger destroyed the demon's home. When it tried to come back, it had no place to which it could return.

The following testimony illustrates how my wife, Denise, overcame a demon that had been afflicting her. She was healed of severe pain from a herniated lumbar disc only after she came to the realization that she had wrong thoughts about the symptoms and God's desire to heal her. Her mindset and spoken words were allowing the enemy to attack her and keep her in pain.

The first problem was that she couldn't believe she was healed as long as she felt pain. Although this statement may seem absurd on its face, it's a common issue with supernatural healing. Sometimes, we feel pain in response to a physiological injury, while other times, the pain is due only to the presence of a spirit. My wife's MRI showed one herniated and two bulging discs. One would think that as long as she had herniated discs, she must live with pain. But we know people who have had MRIs showing herniated discs, and they have no pain. It's as if they have no injury at all. Denise wondered, "If some people have herniated discs and are without pain, why can't I be one of them?"

The second problem was that she wasn't convinced that God wanted her healed. One day, she changed her mind and decided to believe that God did want her healed, and she entertained the idea that perhaps she was already healed. She accepted the fact that her beliefs prevented her healing from manifesting. She also chose to see the pain as a lie from the enemy. That day, she listened to a video where a man prayed for his audience to be healed. Because her thinking had been corrected, it removed the power the enemy had over her, and her faith appropriated her healing. After listening to the man's prayer, she found herself pain-free for the first time in many months. Over the next few weeks, the pain, which was caused by an evil spirit, occasionally returned. But each time it did, she told herself she was healed and commanded the spirit of pain to leave. Each time she did, the pain left. She is still healed today.

An enemy only has the power over us that we allow it to have. Being healed and keeping the symptoms from returning is a battle. Most of the warfare is waged in the battlefield of the mind. Any time the symptoms of disease or pain return, it's likely due to the work of an evil spirit. Command the demon to leave (exercise authority), believe you are healed (demonstrate faith), and consider the need for emotional healing. The next chapter outlines the emotional healing process that I recommend.

Exercise

Find someone with chronic pain who has received prayer but has not been healed. Get permission to pray for them and to deal with spirits that may be causing their symptoms. Ask the person to rate their level of pain. Ask the Holy Spirit to show you if an evil spirit is present. Whether you sense an evil spirit or not, using an authoritative command, tell all evil spirits to leave. Recheck the person's level of pain. Continue commanding evil spirits to leave and rechecking the level of pain until the pain is gone.

CHAPTER NINE

Emotional Healing

THE EXERCISE OF AUTHORITY IS effective for removing evil spirits. But if a demon's home remains intact, it is likely to return. Emotional healing destroys demonic homes and prevents evil spirits from returning. The emotional healing process is simple. This chapter provides a biblical foundation for the concept and a brief explanation of the process.

When an emotionally traumatic event happens, particularly when we are young, our soul can be wounded. A child does not have the coping skills of an adult. What may seem like a silly prank to an adult can actually terrify a young child. The soul of a child is easily damaged by emotional trauma. Spirits of pain and sickness will attach to emotional wounds in the soul that are caused by trauma. If we remove the negative emotion and heal the wound in the soul, evil spirits have one less place they can occupy. In many cases, once the emotional trauma is healed, an evil spirit will leave of its own volition.

Let's examine one of the most well-known verses about healing found in the Old Testament:

He is despised and rejected by men,
A Man of sorrows and acquainted with grief.
And we hid, as it were, our faces from Him;
He was despised, and we did not esteem Him.
Surely He has borne our griefs
And carried our sorrows;
Yet we esteemed Him stricken,
Smitten by God, and afflicted.
But He was wounded for our transgressions,
He was bruised for our iniquities;
The chastisement for our peace was upon Him,
And by His stripes we are healed.
ISA. 53:3-5

In this passage, a prophecy is given that the torture of the Messiah (Jesus) would provide a way for us to be healed. This idea is usually applied to physical healing, but Isaiah suggested that it applied to emotional healing as well. He wrote: "Surely He has borne our griefs and carried our sorrows." Grief and sorrow are painful emotions caused by trauma. If Jesus has borne them for us, we no longer need to bear them. Emotional healing is a matter of allowing Him to take our painful emotions. The approach I use is to have people ask Jesus to take their sadness, rejection, anger, or any other negative emotion and heal the wound it caused in their soul.

With the help of the Holy Spirit, I developed a simple process that is effective and can be done by anyone without the need for special training. I've written a short book titled *Emotional Healing in 3 Easy Steps* that describes the process I used to help a patient who was psychologically distressed. Here are the basic steps for healing emotional trauma which you can use to heal your own emotional wounds or to help others:

1. Identify an event from the past that causes a strong negative emotion when you think of it.
2. Identify the emotion(s) you feel.
3. Ask Jesus to take the emotions from you.

4. Ask Him to heal the wound(s) in your soul.
5. Tell Him you receive His healing.

An optional step is asking Jesus to give you a positive emotion when He removes a negative one. Ask Him to give you joy when He removes sadness, love when He removes hate, and acceptance when He removes rejection.

After you've done this once, recall the event again and see if a negative emotion remains. If there is still a negative emotion, repeat the steps.

1. Identify the emotion(s) you feel.
2. Ask Jesus to take them from you.
3. Ask Him to heal the wound(s) in your soul.
4. Tell Him you receive His healing.

Allow a minute to pass and recall the event again. If a different emotion is present, repeat the process one more time. If a negative emotion is not present, you are healed of the trauma from that event. Consider starting the process again using a different event that evokes a negative emotion when you think of it. Continue using this process until all the trauma that occurred during your life has been healed. In many cases, mysterious illnesses and pains that have not responded to prayer will spontaneously resolve.

If you cannot recall an event that causes a negative emotion, that's not a problem. Jesus doesn't heal the memory. He heals the wound in your soul and removes the negative emotion. So, you can omit step number one from the list above. Don't worry about recalling the event. Identify the emotion you feel and give it to Jesus, then repeat as needed.

The question is often asked: can we be healed of more than one emotion at a time?

Generally, the emotions of a particular event, although different in nature, can be addressed simultaneously. For example, anger, shame, and guilt from a single traumatic event may be healed at once. Sometimes, Jesus will heal the same emotion from different events at the same time. I've also received testimonies from people who have had a variety of emotions from different events healed simultaneously. Some have found that if you find the first occurrence of a negative emotion and heal the wound associated with it, the individual will be healed of all other wounds connected to that emotion. For reasons only He knows, Jesus will use different approaches with different people.

Sometimes, when being healed of emotional trauma, a person will feel a demon lift off of them. Chronic pain syndromes may spontaneously resolve after emotional healing since pain is often caused by the presence of a demon. If symptoms of pain or sickness persist after emotional healing, it may be because a demon is still present. After emotional healing, you can use your authority and command the spirit to leave. The symptoms may change. Sometimes, they will intensify. In other cases, they will subside, but only partially. As long as the symptoms remain, continue with emotional healing and commanding evil spirits to leave.

A general approach is to do a session of emotional healing and then command evil spirits to leave. Take a few minutes and check to see if your symptoms or mood have changed. You can then start another session of emotional healing. When it is complete, command demons to leave. Emotional healing and deliverance may take weeks or months to complete. With severe trauma, it can take years. Be patient. Allow the Holy Spirit to identify specific soul wounds that need healing and address them as they're brought up. In time, you should notice a change in your mood and fewer symptoms of pain and sickness.

CHAPTER TEN

Power for Miracles

JESUS GAVE HIS DISCIPLES THE power to work creative miracles and heal diseases. This chapter will examine that power at work.

> *When they had crossed over, they came to the land of Gennesaret and anchored there. And when they came out of the boat, immediately the people recognized Him, ran through that whole surrounding region, and began to carry about on beds those who were sick to wherever they heard He was. Wherever He entered, into villages, cities, or the country, they laid the sick in the marketplaces, and begged Him that they might just touch the hem of His garment. And as many as touched Him were made well.*
> MARK 6:53-56

Two things are worth noting in this account: When Jesus stepped from the boat, the people immediately recognized Him and went to get anyone who was sick so they might be healed. The townspeople had an expectancy—they knew of the miracles He had worked, and they believed (they had confidence) that He would perform more of them. Faith was abundant in these villages. As with authority, it is faith that releases power for miracles. There was so much faith that merely touching the Lord's garment made the sick well.

Consider the way the sick were healed in this passage. Jesus gave no commands. He didn't cast out demons. The passage reads: "And as many as touched Him were made well." The sick touched Jesus. Power flowed from His body which healed their diseases.

Power for miracles is generally released from one person to another. In the accounts found in the Bible, it is usually done through touch. Let's look at another example from Luke chapter eight:

> *But as He went, the multitudes thronged Him. Now a woman, having a flow of blood for twelve years, who had spent all her livelihood on physicians and could not be healed by any, came from behind and touched the border of His garment. And immediately her flow of blood stopped.*
>
> *And Jesus said, "Who touched Me?"*
>
> *When all denied it, Peter and those with him said, "Master, the multitudes throng and press You, and You say, 'Who touched Me?'"*
>
> *But Jesus said, "Somebody touched Me, for I perceived power going out from Me." Now when the woman saw that she was not hidden, she came trembling; and falling down before Him, she declared to Him in the presence of all the people the reason she had touched Him and how she was healed immediately.*
>
> *And He said to her, "Daughter, be of good cheer; your faith has made you well. Go in peace."*
> LUKE 8:42B-48

In this passage, the woman believed (she was confident) that if she touched the hem of the Lord's garment, she would be healed. Jesus confirmed that power had left Him and noted that the woman's faith made her well. To summarize: the woman was healed when Jesus released power. The mechanism that releases power is faith. Sometimes, the faith of the healer. Other times it is the faith of the receiver.

Let's look at one more example of Jesus healing the sick by releasing power. This account is found in Matthew chapter eight:

> *When He had come down from the mountain, great multitudes followed Him. And behold, a leper came and worshiped Him, saying, "Lord, if You are willing, You can make me clean."*
>
> *Then Jesus put out His hand and touched him, saying, "I am willing; be cleansed." Immediately his leprosy was cleansed.*
> MATT. 8:1-3

These passages illustrate the fact that a release of power can work miracles. How does one receive this power?

After He was raised from the dead, but before He ascended into heaven, Jesus told His disciples to remain in Jerusalem because God the Father would give them power.

> *"Behold, I send the Promise of My Father upon you; but tarry in the city of Jerusalem until you are endued with power from on high."*
> LUKE 24:49

Jesus affirmed that His disciples would receive the power of God. Ten days after He ascended into heaven, on the day of Pentecost, the Holy Spirit was released, and they were filled with God's Spirit:

> *When the Day of Pentecost had fully come, they were all with one accord in one place. And suddenly there came a sound from heaven, as of a rushing mighty wind, and it filled the whole house where they were sitting. Then there appeared to them divided tongues, as of fire, and one sat upon each of them. And they were all filled with the Holy Spirit and began to speak with other tongues, as the Spirit gave them utterance.*
> ACTS 2:1-4

When a disciple of Jesus is born again, the Spirit of God takes up residence in them. The Holy Spirit dwelling in us makes it possible to work miracles. In the same way that Jesus released power for miracles, we can unleash the power of God through direct contact with others.

After they had received the Holy Spirit, the disciples continued healing as Jesus commanded them. Word of the miracles spread throughout the region, and people brought their sick friends and relatives into the streets, hoping they would be healed:

> *And believers were increasingly added to the Lord, multitudes of both men and women, so that they brought the sick out into the streets and laid them on beds and couches, that at least the shadow of Peter passing by might fall on some of them.*
> ACTS 5:14-15

This passage says that people brought out the sick with the hope that the shadow of Peter might fall on them. It doesn't say that Peter's shadow healed the sick. It says people *believed* his shadow had healing power.

Why would they come to this conclusion?

The sick were healed when the disciples passed near them. We know that power went out from Jesus as He passed through a crowd, and the sick were healed. After being filled with the Holy Spirit, the disciples released power for miracles just as He did.

God created a system for working miracles that can be thought of as a power grid. He is the source of power. We are the transmission lines that carry His power into the world. We receive power from Him and it flows into others. This power is the energy needed to repair damaged or diseased body parts or create new ones. To explain how God's power works, I'll use an analogy that examines how electricity provides power for tools and household appliances.

Tools and appliances require different amounts of power to operate them. The power a device uses is described in terms of watts. A standard incandescent light bulb consumes 60 watts of power. An electric coffeemaker might use 600 watts of power, while a table saw might use 1,800 watts. If a power source supplies 100 watts of electricity, it can power a light bulb, but not a coffeemaker or table saw. If a power source delivered 2,000 watts, it could power all three.

Power lines are not equal in their ability to transmit energy. The amount of power a transmission line can carry is determined by its diameter. A larger diameter line can carry more power than a smaller one made of the same material. This is so because a smaller line has greater resistance to the flow of electricity.

The capacity to carry God's power is an important factor to consider. It stands to reason that all humans have approximately the same potential for carrying and releasing God's power. But our *potential* is not the same as the *actual* amount of power we carry at a given time. Faith and unbelief affect the way in which God's power flows through us. Faith enhances the flow of power, while unbelief resists it. It was unbelief that kept the disciples from healing the demon-possessed boy. And faith appropriated the miracle for the woman with the flow of blood.

When I pray for people to be healed, they often feel heat or tingling in the affected area. This suggests, though it does not prove, that power or energy is being released into their body. Their nervous system senses the release of energy from me just as if an electric current or heat lamp had been applied to their skin.

Although power is often transferred through touch, direct contact isn't necessary. Power for miracles can travel over some distance. If my hand is in direct contact with a person's skin, they might attribute the sensation of heat to the warmth radiating from my skin. But if my hand is a few inches from their skin and they note a sensation of heat, it can't be attributed to that. The power for miracles is spiritual power. In the physical world, distance affects the amount of power that can be released. But there is no limit to the distance over which spiritual power can travel. Someone can release power (by faith) from their home in America to heal someone in Africa just as effectively as if they were in the same room together.

Knowing that we do not all have the same degrees of faith and unbelief, it's reasonable to suppose we do not release the same amount of power. Through all my years of experience in healing and in watching others practice and grow, I've noticed that not all injuries require the same amount of power to affect healing. I want to propose a theory as to why this is so. Bones are made of dense tissue that is relatively difficult to break. Ligaments are made of soft connective tissue that can be damaged more easily. Therefore, it seems safe to say that it would require more force (energy) to break a femur bone than to strain a knee ligament. It logically follows that it would require more power to repair a broken femur than a strained knee ligament.

What follows is an illustration for the purpose of teaching. The numbers used in this analogy are not based on clinical research. I don't know how much power is needed to heal a particular condition, and I don't know how much power is released when we pray. This example is offered as a concrete way to understand the abstract principles at work when power is released.

Let's imagine a sprained knee requires ten watts of power to be released before it is healed. A person who can release five watts of power would need two attempts to heal the injury. Someone who releases ten watts of power would only need one attempt. Let's imagine that healing a broken femur requires the release of thirty watts of power. Someone who released five watts of power would need six attempts. Someone who releases ten watts would need three attempts, and a person with great faith who releases fifty watts would need one attempt. If healing Lou Gehrig's disease required two hundred watts of power, the person who releases five watts would need forty attempts. The person who releases ten watts would need twenty attempts. Someone who released fifty watts would need four attempts.

The power we release on a given day and for a particular task is determined by several factors—the most important of which is our level of faith.

We decide that we want to release power for a miracle. We believe that we *will* release power when it is needed. And our belief (confidence) acts as a trigger. The power of God that resides in us flows into those who need healing. Our level of faith (or unbelief) determines the amount of power released.

It is not necessary to know the names of the various parts of the body in order to release power for miracles. I know people who operate effectively in healing and who have very little knowledge of anatomy. However, my medical training required me to learn human anatomy, and God often has me focus on certain anatomical structures. In the section that follows, I'll provide strategies for healing certain conditions, and I'll list the specific body parts that require healing. While this information is not essential, some may find it helpful.

I'm often asked to pray for people who have peripheral neuropathy: a condition affecting the nerves in the hands, arms, feet, and legs. Typical symptoms are numbness, tingling, burning, pain, and eventually, a loss of sensation in the extremities. I've seen many people healed of this condition. I've learned that with neuropathy, the exercise of authority isn't usually required. It responds well to the release of power, which does not require an authoritative command. I place my hands on or near the affected body part, and in my mind, I believe I am releasing the power of God to work a miracle. After a few minutes, I'll ask the person to check their level of sensation. Usually, they will note a change. I keep my hands in the same position and continue believing that the power of God is going into their body. After a few more minutes, I ask the individual to recheck their symptoms. Sometimes, I'll command the nerves to be healed or come back to life, but generally, I remain silent. In most of the cases where I've used this approach, significant improvement is noticed within a few minutes. A healing session may last fifteen or twenty minutes. Complete restoration of damaged nerves can usually be accomplished in a couple of sessions, depending on the severity of the disease and the faith of the individual.

The same approach discussed above can be used to heal degenerative joint disease. When cartilage and other connective tissues are damaged, a release of power will create new tissue.

The meniscus is a pad of cartilage that acts as a shock absorber in the knee joint. With age or overuse, it becomes torn and fails to provide a cushion between the upper and lower leg bones. Symptoms are pain, tenderness, and crepitus (a crunching noise) when flexing the joint. What is needed is new cartilage. To release power for a creative miracle, I'll hold my hands on or near the affected knee. (I use both hands if the right and left knees are affected). In my mind, I believe I am releasing power. My faith (confidence) activates the power of God, which flows into the injured joint, creating new cartilage. The individual may sense heat or tingling, but not always. If they sense heat or tingling, it's a reliable predictor of healing, but I've seen many people healed who felt nothing as power was released.

I employ a similar but slightly different approach with frozen shoulders and torn rotator cuffs. The rotator cuff is cartilage in the shoulder joint that can deteriorate with age, injury, and overuse. When someone suffers a painful shoulder injury, they tend to limit the use of it, which decreases the intensity and frequency of pain but leads to the development of scar tissue that causes a limited range of motion. Over time, the individual may develop a frozen shoulder (also called adhesive capsulitis).

Two different problems must be addressed. The first is the deteriorated cartilage, which requires a creative miracle. The second is the removal of adhesions and scar tissue by exercising authority. Previously, we learned that the exercise of authority can remove things that are not supposed to be present. Typically, it is used to remove demons, but it can also be used to remove scar tissue, tumors, and bacteria that cause infection.

Either condition can be addressed first, or they can be addressed at the same time. As with other conditions, I place my hand on or near the affected shoulder. In my mind, I believe I'm releasing power for a creative miracle to create new cartilage. At the same time, I will command scar tissue to dissolve or disappear. Every few minutes, I'll ask the individual if they feel a change, and I'll have them test their range of motion compared to before I began. As long as I see changes, I'll continue releasing power and commanding scar tissue to dissolve until they are completely healed.

Blindness is usually due to missing or damaged structures in the eye or a damaged or missing optic nerve. A release of power can create new structures in the body. I once prayed for a patient who was blind in both eyes. I used an approach similar to the one described above. I held my hands near the woman's eyes and commanded them to see, and I commanded the eye structures to be made new. I believed I was releasing God's power. Every few minutes, I asked if she noticed any changes. She reported seeing "pools of light" forming in her field of view—something she had never experienced before. As long as I kept my hands near her eyes and commanded them to see, the pools of light became larger, and eventually, she could make out shapes. Her eyes were being healed.

At the time of this encounter, I didn't understand how power for miracles was released. My habit was placing my hands near the affected body part and making appropriate commands. I was releasing power and exercising authority simultaneously, though I did not understand them as being two distinct and different dynamics. It's possible this woman's eyes would have been healed with a release of power alone. Perhaps, authoritative commands were not needed. Not knowing with certainty which was needed, I routinely chose to do both. I don't think it hurts to exercise authority and release power as a matter of habit, and it seems a prudent approach when we aren't sure which one is needed.

Years ago, when I was a paramedic, I became friends with a man who was diagnosed with Lou Gehrig's disease. When I met him, he was paralyzed from his head to his toes. He was capable of blinking his eyes but had no other voluntary muscle movement. Because he could not chew or swallow, he received nutrition through a gastric tube. I decided I would try to get him healed.

He lived in a skilled nursing facility, and, as part of my job, I happened to transport him from time to time to one hospital or another for various health problems. Each time I transported him, I spent a few minutes releasing power into his body and commanding it to be healed. Occasionally, when I was not on duty, I would drive to the facility where he lived and spend twenty to thirty minutes releasing power and exercising authority. I did this for about a year and a half before I moved out of the state. His devoted wife and family were very attentive and welcomed my prayers. They also prayed daily for his healing.

It can be difficult to pray for someone over a long period of time without seeing results. How do I avoid discouragement? I know that discouragement is a tactic of the enemy, so I refuse to entertain thoughts of defeat. I also know it is God's will to heal, and I've found that when I reflect on the miracles I've already seen, my faith remains intact.

One day, I visited my friend expecting to pray for him, but his wife met me at the door and told me of a sudden change. That morning, he was able to sip a little coffee and eat a slice of pizza. He had gradually regained the use of the muscles in his neck and face. They had no explanation—except for prayer.

This experience taught me that, indeed, some conditions require more power to be released than others. In these cases, we must be persistent and release power in successive healing sessions if we want to see miracles. In my friend's case, I was unsure if power or authority was indicated, so I opted for both.

Releasing power to work creative miracles contradicts what many of us have been taught about healing. While the process may fly in the face of conventional wisdom, if you understand the basic concept and practice it, in time, you'll be amazed at the results.

Exercise

Find someone who needs healing of a joint injury. Ask if you may pray with them. Have them rate their pain on a scale from one to ten and have them check their range of motion. Place your hand near the injury and, in your mind, believe you are releasing the power of God. After a few minutes, ask them if they feel anything. Have them rate their level of pain and check their range of motion. Repeat as needed; be aware of the time constraints and comfort level of the person who needs healing.

CHAPTER ELEVEN

Faith

As WE'VE SEEN IN THE previous chapters, the secret to releasing power and exercising authority is faith. And while the concept may appear simple at first glance, the way faith works in the realm of the miraculous remains a mystery to most people. If the proper application of faith was easy, everyone would be doing it. Let's explore this enigma further.

I've often had people tell me they have faith, and yet, when they pray, people are not healed. The problem is a misunderstanding of the biblical concept of faith. To begin this chapter, let's have another look at a passage from Matthew chapter 17 that was discussed previously. When they were not able to heal a boy with epilepsy, the disciples of Jesus asked why:

> *Then the disciples came to Jesus privately and said, "Why could we not cast it out?"*

So, Jesus said to them, "Because of your unbelief; for assuredly,
I say to you, if you have faith as a mustard seed, you will say to
this mountain, 'Move from here to there,' and it will move; and
nothing will be impossible for you."
MATT. 17:19-20

The disciples could not cast out the demon because of their unbelief.
Put differently; they lacked faith. But it wasn't as though they were
completely faithless. On the contrary, they had already experienced
some degree of success. But this failure caught them by surprise, thus
their question to Jesus.

He said if they had faith as a mustard seed, they could move mountains. Some teach that Jesus spoke of the *size* of their faith when He
compared it to a mustard seed. The idea is that small faith can move
mountains—if it is pure or has some other quality. But Jesus didn't
use size in this comparison. He didn't say they needed to have faith as
small as a mustard seed. Rather, He said they needed faith that *acts*
the way a mustard seed acts.

How does a mustard seed act?

In the kingdom parables of Matthew chapter 13, Jesus likened the
kingdom of heaven to a mustard seed:

"The kingdom of heaven is like a mustard seed, which a man took
and sowed in his field, which indeed is the least of all the seeds;
but when it is grown it is greater than the herbs and becomes
a tree, so that the birds of the air come and nest in its branches."
MATT. 13:31-32

Although the mustard seed is small, in this parable, it grew into a large
tree. A seed bears no fruit until it germinates and grows into a plant.
The larger the plant, the more fruit it bears. Faith must grow before it
produces the fruit of healing and miracles.

I had been an atheist for most of my life. After I came to believe that
Jesus was my Savior, I still had no faith for the miraculous. I was
taught that healing and miracles ceased centuries ago. But one night, in

a dream, I received a promise from God; "I want you to pray for your patients, and I'll heal them." I had been given a seed of promise. So, I obeyed God to the best of my ability. For several months, I begged Him to heal my patients. During that time, I saw no miracles. But the kingdom of God is about growth, so I planted the seed and watered it. I watched videos where people prayed for others to be healed, and I witnessed miracles. The seed sprouted. I watered it with scripture and read every account of healing in the Bible. The seed grew roots. God gave me dreams in which I saw myself praying for the sick, and they were healed. Leaves grew from a small stalk that emerged from the ground. I continued laying hands on anyone who would let me, and eventually, I saw a few people healed. Fruit began to appear.

I misunderstood faith for healing and how it operates. Most of you would call yourselves Christians, disciples of Jesus, or simply "believers." You believe certain things about Jesus—the most important of which is that He is your Savior. This type of faith is the kind that saves us from the consequences of sin, but it's not the kind that heals the sick or works miracles. Every Christian believes that Jesus is their Savior, but few operate in the miraculous.

The kind of faith that releases power isn't a belief that God *wants* to heal the sick. Many people believe that God wants to heal the sick, and yet, the sick are not healed when they pray. Faith for healing and miracles is different from this.

Some people equate faith with "hope" or "wishful thinking." Faith for the miraculous is not hope. Hope implies that both a degree of optimism and uncertainty are present in one's mind. Faith for the miraculous is devoid of uncertainty. It is absolute, unshakable confidence.

The faith that is needed to exercise authority or release power for miracles consistently is the belief (confidence) that when you are presented with an opportunity to release power for a miracle or exercise authority, that the power of God that is in you will, in fact, be released and heal the particular condition in the individual who needs it. Faith that heals consistently is not general. It is *specific* to the person who is sick, the condition being addressed, and the one who is praying. Allow me to illustrate this further.

When the woman was healed by taking hold of the hem of Jesus' garment, Jairus was in the crowd looking on. His daughter was sick, and he came to Jesus for help. After the woman was healed, Jesus had her testify to the crowd. After she testified, a friend of Jairus appeared and informed him that his daughter had died. Jesus looked at Jairus and said, "Do not be afraid; only believe, and she will be made well" (see Luke 8:40-50).

The woman's testimony was needed because Jesus wanted Jairus to hear it and have faith for something specific. Believing that He is the Messiah was important, but He was after something else. He didn't want Jairus to believe that God heals some people or that He raises some people from the dead. He wanted Jairus to believe without a doubt that *his own* daughter would be raised from the dead. Note that Jesus said the girl would be made well *if* he believed. The faith that Jairus needed if his daughter were to be resurrected was specific to *his* daughter and *her* condition. This is the kind of faith we need to exercise authority and release power for miracles.

I'd like to bring clarity to the issue of faith in the general sense and explain how it differs from specific faith. When I began praying with people for healing, I seldom expected any of them to be healed. Although I believed that God wanted to heal some people and some conditions, I did not believe He wanted to heal them all. I had a generalized faith in the idea of healing. To make matters worse, I thought the person I was praying with would not be healed. I had other doubts, too. Those doubts involved either the person for whom I was praying or the condition for which I was praying. I doubted that God wanted to heal everyone, and I believed He would heal just about anyone *except* the person with whom I was praying. Because I didn't know that God wanted to heal everyone, my faith was generalized to some people and some conditions, but it was not specific to the one I was praying with or their condition. So, when I prayed for specific people with specific conditions, my doubts surfaced, and I imagined them not being healed. My specific doubts destroyed my generalized faith, and no one was healed.

After months of fruitless attempts at healing, I realized I had to change my approach. I noticed that some people commanded healing instead of asking God to heal and that this approach seemed to work well.

I changed my method and started commanding healing. When I did, I saw people healed. Often, they were healed instantly. Before long, I saw decent success with people who had torn rotator cuffs and carpal tunnel syndrome. Because I was seeing people consistently healed of these two conditions, I approached them with more confidence (faith). After only a few more months, I'd seen dozens of people healed with a success rate for these conditions of around 90 percent. Because of that success, I started to believe (I had confidence) that God would heal everyone I prayed with who had one of these two conditions. My faith, which was generalized until then, became specific. There were certain people with certain conditions that I knew in my heart, without any doubt, would be healed. It was at this point that before praying with people, I told them they would be healed. I had greater faith for some conditions than others. My doubt about specific conditions was gradually being removed. And my faith for just about every type of condition was greater than it had been.

As I began praying for people with neurological disorders like Parkinson's, multiple sclerosis, and ALS (Lou Gehrig's), I found that I had little faith. But, in time, I saw a few people healed of these conditions. As a result, my confidence grew, and my success with these conditions gradually improved. The same was true for cancer.

Like many people, my confidence for seeing cancer healed was small at first. I saw cancer as a stronger adversary. But as I prayed with more cancer patients, I saw some of them healed, and my faith for healing this condition grew quickly. Today, I have about the same faith for healing cancer that I do for joint injuries.

Like the faith of Jairus, my faith was strengthened by watching God's power at work. Faith must grow. Seeing people healed is one of the keys to growth. There is no substitute for witnessing the power of God at work.

The strategy for growing your faith is to start with a generalized belief that God heals, raises the dead, and wants demons removed. From there, you lay hands on whomever you can, and eventually, you'll see some of them healed. The same principle applies to deliverance, raising the dead, and working miracles. As you gain experience, your weak, generalized faith will become more specific and stronger, and you'll see certain diseases healed and demons evicted. You'll develop greater faith for specific situations. As you persist, your strong faith for a few situations will broaden into a strong faith for many of them.

Exercise

Faith grows with practice. For this exercise, I'll ask you to release power or exercise authority as described in the previous chapters. Find several people who need healing and work with them over a length of time. It may help to begin to visualize them being healed before you pray—turning doubt away. As you practice releasing power and exercising authority, you should become more confident that people will be healed when you pray for them.

CHAPTER TWELVE

The Gift of Faith

SOMETIMES, WE WON'T HAVE THE faith necessary to release power or exercise authority successfully. Fortunately, God has anticipated this problem and made a way for us to obtain greater faith supernaturally. The mechanism is described in the apostle Paul's first letter to the church in Corinth. In chapter 12, Paul describes the gifts of the Holy Spirit. He notes that the gifts are "manifestations of the Spirit." The gifts are ways in which the Spirit of God makes known to us (manifests) His nature:

> *There are diversities of gifts, but the same Spirit. There are differences of ministries, but the same Lord. And there are diversities of activities, but it is the same God who works all in all. But the manifestation of the Spirit is given to each one for the profit of all: for to one is given the word of wisdom through the Spirit, to another the word of knowledge through the same Spirit, to another faith by the same Spirit, to another gifts of healings by the same*

Spirit, to another the working of miracles, to another prophecy, to another discerning of spirits, to another different kinds of tongues, to another the interpretation of tongues. But one and the same Spirit works all these things, distributing to each one individually as He wills.
1 COR. 12:4-11

Paul explained that faith is a gift of the Holy Spirit. When we lack faith, we can ask God for more. One way we can receive it is through the operation of the Holy Spirit. In the same way that God gives us power we do not normally possess, He can give us greater faith.

Naturally, we would think that a gift is something we receive from another. Once we receive it, the gift becomes ours, like a birthday gift from a friend. However, a friend does not live inside of us, but the Spirit of God does. Because we have God's Spirit living in us, His gifts are not given *to us* as much as they are operational *in us*.

The way in which Paul listed the gifts of the Spirit might make it seem as if only one gift is given to each believer: "To one is given the word of wisdom through the Spirit, to another the word of knowledge through the same Spirit." However, I don't believe Paul meant to imply that the gifts are limited in their distribution numerically. Rather, he described the diversity of gifts as they are distributed to all believers.

In the fourteenth chapter of his letter, Paul wrote that we should desire spiritual gifts, especially the gift of prophecy:

Pursue love, and desire spiritual gifts, but especially that you may prophesy. For he who speaks in a tongue does not speak to men but to God, for no one understands him; however, in the spirit he speaks mysteries. But he who prophesies speaks edification and exhortation and comfort to men.
1 COR. 14:1-3

If believers were limited to only one spiritual gift, Paul would not have instructed us to desire other ones. In verse 31 of the same chapter, he wrote, "For you can all prophesy one by one, that all may learn and all may be encouraged." If all believers may prophesy, we may operate in the other gifts as well, including the gift of faith. Because the Spirit of God lives in us, at any time, we may operate in any spiritual gift. God can *manifest* through us whatever gift is needed for a particular situation. In addition to the gifts of prophecy and faith, the gifts of healings and miracles can operate in us at any time.

One day, I received a healing testimony by email that illustrates how the gift of faith operates. Here is part of the testimony:

> I listened to your recent Spiritual Q & A podcast, and Alan's testimony, which brought up the connection between pain and demons attaching themselves to our bodies, to cause us illness and pain. For some reason—Holy Spirit, no doubt—I decided to use this idea, to cure myself of a going-on-for three year fistula on my anus.
>
> My life had been miserable for some time, thanks to this ailment, and things had got so bad that I'd had to plan any trips from the house (even to local shops) so that I could be close to an available toilet. I absolutely dreaded leaving home, even to bring my 80+ year old parents for medical check-ups.
>
> And then I heard yourself and Alan on your podcast, at the beginning of this month. Cue Margaret V Anal Demon (as I called it). And so, I bound, I rebuked, and I cast off that Anal Demon in the Holy Name of Jesus, my Redeemer, and my Saviour; my eternal Healer. I imagined and called out the words that I bathed my parts in Jesus' Holy Blood; a single drop would cure me forever. I just let the words come, Dave.
>
> The surge of absolute belief that ran through me felt like I was suddenly made of metal. I felt a fury I'd never felt before, white hot and absolute. I continued this practice, each time I had to use the loo. I never felt that white hot furious absoluteness again, after that first time, but within two days, I saw an improvement in my condition. My bottom began to feel like its old self (it was returning to its proper shape, as the fistula disappeared). Yep, nine days after I first heard your podcast, I write to you completely and utterly healed. The fistula has disappeared completely. Leakage—gone. Boils and pimples—gone. That constant got-to-go-now urge—gone. That need to be near a toilet—gone. My life has returned, for the first time in nearly three years! I have no need for salve. No more wadding. No more 'accidents' because I can't get to a loo quickly enough. I no longer dread wiping or washing and cleaning myself.

I'd like to highlight a couple of points from this testimony. First, note this statement: "The surge of absolute belief that ran through me felt like I was suddenly made of metal. I felt a fury I'd never felt before, white hot and absolute." The writer suddenly experienced greater faith ("absolute belief") than she'd ever had before. This supernatural faith worked together with her authoritative commands to remove the demon and its disease. But how did she develop this faith? The answer is found in this statement: "For some reason—Holy Spirit, no doubt—I decided to use this idea, to cure myself..."

The Holy Spirit gave her the idea to use this principle to heal herself and then gave her the faith required to make it happen. This is how the gift of faith operates. When we lack the faith needed for healing, deliverance, or a creative miracle, we can ask God to give us the faith that is needed. Then, with our newfound faith, we can release the power or exercise the authority needed to address the problem.

Exercise

Think of a situation where you have prayed but have not seen success. Ask the Holy Spirit to give you the faith needed to prevail in this situation. Take whatever actions the Holy Spirit leads you to take and observe the results.

CHAPTER THIRTEEN

Raising the Dead

THE SAME POWER AND AUTHORITY for healing sickness and removing demons can be used to raise the dead. Previously, we looked at the account of the woman who was healed after touching the hem of Jesus' garment. A man named Jairus (the leader of a synagogue) looked on with hope as she was healed because his own daughter was sick, and he hoped Jesus would heal her. Here is the account from Luke chapter eight that immediately follows her healing:

> *While He was still speaking, someone came from the ruler of the synagogue's house, saying to him, "Your daughter is dead. Do not trouble the Teacher."*
>
> *But when Jesus heard it, He answered him, saying, "Do not be afraid; only believe, and she will be made well." When He came into the house, He permitted no one to go in except Peter, James,*

*and John, and the father and mother of the girl. Now all wept and
mourned for her; but He said, "Do not weep; she is not dead, but
sleeping." And they ridiculed Him, knowing that she was dead.*

*But He put them all outside, took her by the hand and called,
saying, "Little girl, arise."*

*Then her spirit returned, and she arose immediately. And He com-
manded that she be given something to eat. And her parents were
astonished, but He charged them to tell no one what had happened.*
LUKE 8:49-56

There is some dispute about whether the girl was, in fact, dead since
Jesus said she was sleeping. Taken literally, there would be no need
for a resurrection. But it seems the Lord was speaking metaphorically.
One verse in this passage says the disciples ridiculed him, knowing
she was dead. Another verse states that the girl's spirit returned. This
would not be possible unless she died. (It's worth considering that the
author of this account, Luke, was a physician.)

How was the girl raised from the dead?

Jesus exercised authority. He told the girl to arise. Her father believed
she would be resurrected. In response to the authority of Christ and
the faith of Jairus, her spirit returned, and she was brought back to
life. This same method was used to raise back to life a man who had
died in the city of Nain:

*Now it happened, the day after, that He went into a city called
Nain; and many of His disciples went with Him, and a large crowd.
And when He came near the gate of the city, behold, a dead man
was being carried out, the only son of his mother; and she was a
widow. And a large crowd from the city was with her. When the
Lord saw her, He had compassion on her and said to her, "Do
not weep." Then He came and touched the open coffin, and those
who carried him stood still. And He said, "Young man, I say to
you, arise." So he who was dead sat up and began to speak. And
He presented him to his mother.*
LUKE 7:11-15

Jesus made an authoritative command, and the dead man's spirit returned. Now, let's look at the way in which He raised Lazarus from the dead. John chapter 11 contains the story of how Lazarus died. Jesus asked the dead man's sisters to take him to the tomb:

Then Jesus, again groaning in Himself, came to the tomb. It was a cave, and a stone lay against it. Jesus said, "Take away the stone."

Martha, the sister of him who was dead, said to Him, "Lord, by this time there is a stench, for he has been dead four days."

Jesus said to her, "Did I not say to you that if you would believe you would see the glory of God?" Then they took away the stone from the place where the dead man was lying. And Jesus lifted up His eyes and said, "Father, I thank You that You have heard Me. And I know that You always hear Me, but because of the people who are standing by I said this, that they may believe that You sent Me." Now when He had said these things, He cried with a loud voice, "Lazarus, come forth!" And he who had died came out bound hand and foot with graveclothes, and his face was wrapped with a cloth. Jesus said to them, "Loose him, and let him go."
JOHN 11:38-44

Once again, an authoritative command was given. The exercise of authority, when done in accordance with the will of God, can raise the dead back to life.

You could try to raise the dead as a matter of protocol. Whenever someone dies, you could command them to return to life. You might see a few people resurrected, but others will remain dead. The question will then be asked: Why are some brought back to life and others are not?

Insight into this matter is found in John chapter 10, where Jesus contrasted His purpose with that of His enemy:

The thief does not come except to steal, and to kill, and to destroy. I have come that they may have life, and that they may have it more abundantly.
JOHN 10:10

89

Jesus came to give us life. The kingdom of darkness wants us dead. This is why demons afflict us with disease and kill us. God allows us to raise people from the dead when the enemy takes their lives prematurely. Resurrection restores them to life so they can accomplish God's purposes.

My friend, Jesse Birkey, who works as a paramedic, has seen several people raised from the dead without the aid of medical equipment. In a couple of cases, he heard the Holy Spirit tell him to command the dead person to come back to life. He obeyed, and they were resurrected.

(Jesse's adventures in dead raising can be found in his book, *"Life Resurrected."*)

Before we attempt to raise someone from the dead, it may be wise to consider if the individual wants to come back to life. Many people have decided they're ready for heaven and may not want to return. We should also ask if it is God's will for someone to return once they've died. The Holy Spirit can tell us when resurrection is appropriate and when it is not.

CHAPTER FOURTEEN

God's Manifest Presence

OCCASIONALLY, GOD WILL SOVEREIGNLY HEAL a person without the need for us to exercise authority or release power. This type of healing is a manifestation of God's *presence.* Some prefer the term *glory.* Let's look at a few Bible passages that shed light on this mysterious concept.

In the days of the kings of Israel, the glory of God rested between the cherubim, on the mercy seat, above the Ark of the testimony in the temple. Then, one day, the prophet Ezekiel witnessed the glory of the Lord as it departed from the temple:

> *So the cherubim lifted up their wings, with the wheels beside them, and the glory of the God of Israel was high above them. And the glory of the LORD went up from the midst of the city and stood on the mountain, which is on the east side of the city.*
> EZEK. 11:22-23

This passage and others like it suggest that God's manifest presence can inhabit a particular area and that it can leave. The seventeenth chapter of the book of John contains a fascinating statement about the glory of God:

> *And the glory which You gave Me I have given them, that they may be one just as We are one: I in them, and You in Me; that they may be made perfect in one, and that the world may know that You have sent Me, and have loved them as You have loved Me.*
> JOHN 17:22-23

The same glory that God the Father gave to Jesus, He has given to us so that we would live in unity the way the Father, the Son, and the Spirit do. Before the death and resurrection of Christ, the temple in Jerusalem was the habitation of the presence of God. But since He ascended into heaven, we have become the temples in which the glory of God dwells.

Years ago, I began listening to the messages of Brian Fenimore, who teaches on the subject of God's presence. He says that we can invite God's presence to come to the location where we are. He teaches that we can sense when His presence comes and when it leaves. This idea seemed strange to me. I wondered: if we carry God's presence, how that same presence can visit us as if it is not already with us?

God's manifest presence acts like the sea. It moves in waves. As it moves, it increases in volume (or intensity) in a given location. But the increase is temporary since His presence always moves from one location to another. A tall wave in the ocean is a visible manifestation of a large volume of water. As a wave passes a fixed location, the volume of water increases, and the wave grows taller. As the volume of water decreases, the wave height decreases, and a trough forms. The trough is the visible manifestation of a decreased volume of water.

On the seashore, pools of water are formed as depressions in the ground retain some of the water from a passing wave. While it is true that a pool contains a certain amount of water, over time, it dissipates. But another passing wave can fill it again. An area that already had some water can receive more. In the same way, we may carry a limited amount of God's glory. But we can receive and sense a greater degree of it as a wave of God's presence passes us. We feel the increase and decrease of His presence as it waxes and wanes.

After hearing Brian Fenimore teach about God's presence, my wife Denise and I spent our evenings inviting God to bring His presence into our home. Each time we did, if I was standing, I swayed gently back and forth uncontrollably. Denise felt a weighty sensation on her body. These sensations came on gradually, lasted a few minutes, and then subsided, much like a passing wave in the ocean.

I then asked God to bring His presence when I prayed for people to be healed. If I was standing, I would gently sway back and forth involuntarily. This would last for several minutes, and then, the phenomenon would cease. One day, I decided to see if God's presence alone would heal people.

While teaching at a school of supernatural ministry a few years ago, I did an experiment. At the end of my lessons, I typically spend time praying for students to be healed. Occasionally, I would ask God to bring His presence and then wait. I would not release power or exercise authority. Instead, I observed the individual to see if God's presence alone would heal them. Sometimes, they would be healed just by being in God's manifest presence.

Based on these experiences, I developed a new model for healing. When I'm asked to pray for someone to be healed, I first ask God to bring His presence. I'll wait until I feel the atmosphere shift, and then, I'll release power or exercise authority.

In a broadcast that I did with Brian, he said that God's presence can manifest in different ways for different purposes. If we need physical healing, we can ask for God's presence for healing. If we're dealing with a demon, we can ask Him to bring His presence for deliverance. We can ask Him to bring His presence for revelation if we want dreams, visions, or words of knowledge. The first time I asked God to bring His presence for revelation, I dreamt the entire night.

For many years, I had suffered from interrupted sleep. I would wake between two and five o'clock in the morning and lie awake for hours.

Brian also said we can invite God's presence for *peace* into our room if we suffer from insomnia. I began a nightly habit of asking God to bring His presence for peace. I also command evil spirits to leave my house and go to the feet of Jesus. For several months afterward, I slept through the night consistently. Sometimes, I'd be so groggy in the morning it was difficult to get out of bed. There was a definite change in my sleep pattern, which continues to this day. I rarely wake in the morning before five o'clock, and most days, I feel well-rested.

Although it isn't a matter of power or authority, learning to cooperate with God and the ways in which He manifests His presence has advantages. One benefit is that God's presence confirms His existence to skeptics. I used to love debating with people about God's existence. I once talked to a co-worker for 12 hours about the existence of God. We covered every theological topic I could bring to my mind. She was happy to talk and listen, but at the end of the day, she was no more convinced of God's existence than before. The apostle Paul said his message did not come in excellence of speech but in the demonstration of God's power (see 1 Cor. 2:4). The power of God was missing from my argument.

Words convey ideas; we need them to communicate theological concepts. But our arguments need evidence. Christians often talk about a personal God who interacts with them. It's one feature that sets ours apart from other belief systems. But when we tell our friends about God, we often forget the personal experience—the evidence. God should show up and do something.

One day, I went to a hairstyling appointment with my wife. She likes having me along because she knows I'll have a few God stories to tell her stylist, Angie, who is open to discussions about God and the supernatural. While she did my wife's hair, we talked about the miraculous. The discussion was going well, so I told her we would show her evidence of God's existence.

I told Angie we would ask God to bring His presence into the room so she could know He was real and experience Him personally. I wanted to prepare her for the experience but didn't want to coach her into feeling something that wasn't God's presence. I explained that we had done this before with my mother-in-law and described what she felt.

I described what God's presence feels like to me, and Denise shared what it feels like to her. We told Angie it's a little different for everyone.

I knew she suffered from chronic neck pain because we had discussed it before. I thought maybe God would heal her neck that night. We stood with our hands out and eyes closed. I asked God's presence to come. After about thirty seconds, I asked Him to bring His power to heal. We waited about two minutes, then opened our eyes and discussed what we felt.

"Wow... that was so weird," Angie said, "as soon as you asked God's presence to come, I felt something like a force pushing me forward. I was thinking to myself, I'm gonna fall over, and I was telling the force, hey, knock it off." I told her that some people do fall over when God's presence is strong. She laughed because she had seen this happen but thought it was people acting weird to get attention.

Then, Angie told us about her pinkie fingers. "I feel a burning sensation in both of my pinkie fingers. It's not uncomfortable; it's just really warm. It started in my fingers and traveled down the outside of my hands and into my wrists." She placed her fingers on her cheeks to see if the heat was real. I asked if she had carpal tunnel syndrome. Her eyes grew bigger, "Yeah, how did you know? I'm ambidextrous, so I have it in both wrists." It seemed to me that God was healing her carpal tunnel problem and not her neck pain, as I had anticipated. This experience became a template that I use when praying in person for people to be healed.

Some have learned to heal the sick by exercising authority alone, independent of God's manifest presence. In this dynamic, healing is a mechanical rather than a relational process. And while it's possible to heal the sick without experiencing God's presence, I don't recommend it. Healing is intended to be relational. When problems arise, if you're in a relationship with the Holy Spirit, you can ask for help. We can ask God to manifest His presence for deliverance if someone is demonically oppressed or to manifest His presence for revelation if we need to know why a certain condition has not been healed. The Holy Spirit will give us keys to healing conditions that would otherwise be incurable, and occasionally; He will heal them sovereignly.

Exercise

Sit in a comfortable chair, or stand in a comfortable position. Close your eyes and ask God to bring His manifest presence. Wait a few minutes and note any sensations you feel or scenes that appear in your mind.

CHAPTER FIFTEEN

Practicing the Art of Healing

WHEN I WATCH A MAJOR league baseball player consistently drive fastballs over the centerfield wall, I wonder how they learned to hit so well. When I watch a master guitarist play a scorching solo, I wonder if I could learn their technique. Jack Nicklaus was asked once how he became such a consistent golfer. He said, "Excellence in golf is a matter of learning how to do a few things extremely well and learning how to do them well consistently."

One might imagine that only a handful of people are born with these extraordinary "gifts," but the truth might surprise you. If you or I put in the time it takes to learn one of these skills, we will eventually master it. Hitting a fastball out of the park, playing a tricky guitar riff, or sinking a fifty-foot putt are nothing more than learning how to do a couple of things well and learning to do them consistently. Anyone can excel in any field they choose. The key to success in anything is practice, practice, practice. The same principle applies to healing and miracles; your consistent practice will be a key.

There are many misunderstandings about how divine healing works. I can't correct every misconception, but two of the main points people get wrong are the idea that God is the one who decides who gets healed and when, and the belief that only a few gifted people can do it.

God does not decide (except in rare cases) who gets healed and when they will be healed. If you think He does, you might go on a field trip with a person who operates successfully in healing. When 90 percent of the people for whom they pray receive healing, it should cause you to re-evaluate your understanding of how healing works. You might even switch from believing that God chooses who gets healed to the equally wrong belief that some people have a special gift for healing.

Here's the truth about how healing works: Jesus gave *every* believer *all* the power and authority they need to heal *anyone* they choose of *any* condition they might have. God has given us everything we need. When someone is not healed, it isn't because God doesn't want them healed. Healing happens when we learn to exercise authority and release power consistently.

How do we learn to release power and exercise authority consistently?

By practicing.

Over the years, I've received hundreds of emails from people asking why, when they pray for themselves, a relative, or a friend, they are not healed. In nearly every case, the individual has limited their attempts exclusively to themselves or those in their immediate circle of friends or family. Their attempts at healing are generally only when someone is in dire need.

If you only pray when a family member or friend is in dire straits, you're unlikely to have success. Most of us require a period of growth where we experience some success and some failure. The successes help our faith grow. Greater faith leads to greater success. When you pray and someone is not healed, you may experience frustration. If it happens often, you may become angry at God. Disappointment over failed attempts to heal people when you're only doing it once in a while is like picking up a guitar a couple of times a year and wondering why you can't play your favorite lick, or standing in the batter's box against a major league pitcher and wondering why you can't hit their fastball.

You'll never have success in healing as long as you're content to do it once in a while. Healing is like an art form that requires instruction, correction, and practice. The best healers are not the ones who are the most gifted. They're the ones who practice the most. Learning to release power is a process, and most people resent the process. We'd rather have God simply heal our friends so we can move on to more exciting things. But that's not how healing works.

Jesus took His disciples out frequently. He demonstrated how to work miracles. He watched as they operated healing and deliverance. He fine-tuned their approach and corrected their mistakes until they became proficient. This is how Jesus taught His disciples, and it's no different today. We have the Holy Spirit as our tutor. Healing, like anything else, must be done over and over until you learn how to do it well and how to do it consistently. In the process of trial and error and in the hours of practice, we eliminate mistakes, grow our faith, and learn the ways of God.

Everyone I know (without exception) who operates proficiently in the miraculous does so because they've committed themselves to making it their lifestyle and not just an occasional thing they do when a friend or relative is in a crisis. The time to learn how to operate in healing and miracles is not when you or your loved one is dying. The best time to prepare for a health emergency is during times of peace. If you set aside a little time each week to practice the art of healing, you'll be amazed at how quickly you'll learn. While learning, some healers see their practice as experimentation; they don't get too invested in the outcome but try different approaches to learn how they can achieve the best results.

CHAPTER SIXTEEN

Protection or Boldness?

I WOULD BE NEGLIGENT IF I did not warn you that when you exercise authority or release power in a way that threatens the kingdom of darkness, that kingdom's servants will oppose you. When Joseph pursued his destiny as revealed to him through dreams, his brothers threw him into a pit. He was sold into slavery and was later framed by an evil woman and imprisoned. After Peter and James healed the sick and told the townspeople about the Messiah, they were thrown in prison. The apostle Paul suffered many attacks as a representative of God's kingdom. Over two millennia, millions of believers have been executed for their faith in Christ.

When the enemy attacks, it's natural to pray to God for protection. Most times, it is warranted. God has supernaturally protected me on many occasions. But some attacks are allowed by God because He wants us to grow in spiritual maturity. Some lessons require us to develop personal strategies and tactics that will help us overcome the enemy. These lessons necessitate an attack by an opponent.

In cases where God permits an attack, we need boldness to withstand the assault. We also need divine wisdom and instruction about which tactics to employ that will help us neutralize the attack. Kris Vallotton shared a story that illustrates this principle:

Over several months, Kris was harassed nightly by a demon that showed up in his bedroom. The demon's antics made it difficult to sleep. After reaching the point of desperation, he asked the Holy Spirit how to handle the situation. The Lord said, "I'm going to show you the power of ignore." The Holy Spirit told him to simply ignore the demon. From that night on, whenever the evil spirit appeared, Kris rolled over in bed and ignored it. Soon, the demon left, and it never returned.

Kris did not need God's protection. Instead, he needed a strategy that would hit the demon in its area of weakness. This particular demon feeds off the attention of its victims. When he gave it no attention, it left to find another victim that would give it what it wanted.

Sometimes, we should pray for divine protection, but if an attack continues, consider the possibility that God may want to give you a strategy to overcome an oppressor.

CHAPTER SEVENTEEN

Rob's Story

I WAS AT WORK WHEN my sister called. She left a message. "Call mom as soon as you can. We have bad news about Rob." The bad news was that my younger brother Rob had just been diagnosed with cancer. But it was worse: Cancer had already spread past the point of being treatable. His doctors felt chemotherapy would be of no use. Their prognosis was that he would die quickly.

I broke the news to my wife. She cried herself to sleep that night. I had already lost my father and one brother to cancer. She was afraid it would eventually come after me. While working the following day, we made plans to fly to North Carolina, where my brother lived. Our main objective was to get him healed.

A couple of friends dropped by before we left. My friend Todd reminded me not to pick a fight with the enemy. Another friend, David, reminded me that I was on business for the kingdom. They prayed for me and then left to carry out their own assignments.

On the flight to Charlotte, I saw Todd in a vision. He taught me how to wage war. He spoke to the disease like he would anyone else. He wasn't angry. He didn't make accusations. Emotionally, he was unmoved. In the vision, he taught me patience in dealing with disease. I sensed no fear in him. Fear is one of the enemy's greatest weapons. As I watched him talk with the disease, I learned that confidence in who I represent is the key to victory.

After picking up our rental car and checking into our hotel room, we met my family at their house. They had a plan. One of us would stay in Rob's hospital room each night to help with his care. Since I was only staying for two days, tomorrow would be my turn. We got caught up on what they knew about his condition and then turned in for the night.

I spent most of the next 24 hours at the hospital, most of it with Rob. I read his chart. His symptoms began five months earlier, but he didn't seek medical treatment until it was too late. He had small-cell carcinoma of the prostate with metastasis to the liver and possibly the pancreas and bladder. He also had DIC (disseminated intravascular coagulopathy), which causes both excessive bleeding and abnormal clotting. He was in a lot of pain, which they managed well.

I prayed as the Spirit led me for most of the morning and afternoon. I typically close my eyes, and God shows me the problems I need to address as images in my mind. I then pray accordingly. I saw tumors, blood clots, cellular structures, demonic beings, damaged organs, and many other things that needed repair. Finally, I saw a bright, golden ball of light traveling through his body from his head to his feet. It seemed to be the healing power of God or at least a representation of it. In the evening, I prayed against depression, pain, and despair. It seemed as if Rob's emotions were under attack. He woke up once every hour. I asked if he was in pain. He always said "yes," so his nurse gave him morphine.

When Rob was admitted, a doctor asked if he was a Christian. He replied that he was an agnostic. When he was awake, he was too sedated for a real conversation. But he did understand simple commands. I told him I had an important thing for him to do. I said, "Jesus is looking for you. I need you to find him." He said, "Okay, I'll look for him."

At two am, I felt like the healing warfare was done. Each time I went back to Rob's bedside to pray, I saw nothing in the way of direction from the Holy Spirit. I began worshiping God and rested in His presence. At four o'clock in the morning, Rob awoke. I asked if he was in pain. He said, "no." I asked again and got the same answer. To make sure he understood the question, I asked if he wanted morphine. He said, "no." He refused morphine the rest of the day. Somehow, his pain had vanished.

Rob's wife came to see him around nine o'clock. When I told her he didn't want morphine, she didn't believe me. Everyone who asked that morning got the same answer. He wasn't in pain. My brothers and sisters came and went. Lost in the blur of activity, I sensed my mission was done, so I went to the house to meet my wife and the rest of my family.

I gave them a report on what happened overnight (without the details of my prayer time). I was full of faith—confident Rob would be healed. We left for the airport and arrived early. I was exhausted, so I dozed in the terminal, but I slept better on the airplane. During the flight, I had another vision.

I saw Rob lying quietly with his eyes closed. As I watched, he slipped into a dark body of water. Then he was gone. My heart sank. I knew what it meant.

The next morning at work, I received the phone call I feared. It was my mother. "Rob died a few minutes ago. Ellie (his wife) is a wreck. Keep her in your prayers."

The Rest of The Story

While discussing Rob's condition with my older brother, he said something that surprised me. Rob had already accepted his death long before I got there. "Rob already said his goodbyes. He's okay with dying. He's ready for whatever comes next." When the doctors told him there was no treatment and he would die shortly, Rob accepted death without a battle.

Books about war contain stories about soldiers who sustained injuries that were survivable, and yet these soldiers died because they believed their wounds to be fatal. There are stories about soldiers who had been ripped in half and shouldn't have survived, but they did. Our will to survive is critical in the realm of both medicine and divine healing. It's nearly impossible to keep a person alive once they've decided it's their time to die.

The same day Rob died, I posted a testimony on my website of a man who was miraculously healed of liver and bladder cancer. That story was scheduled to post two weeks in advance. When the man's doctor told him he had an aggressive form of cancer, this was his reply: "I have a relationship with the greatest healer in all the world. His name is Jesus Christ, and he will heal me." A short time later, he was miraculously healed.

While speaking with one of my older brothers, I also talked with his wife. I heard she had been hospitalized with blood clots in her leg, and I asked her to explain the situation. She had vascular disease in her lower leg for a long time. "My foot has been ice cold for as long as I can remember. There's almost no circulation. The doctors aren't sure what to do about it." I asked if she wanted to be healed. Her eyes lit up. "Yes!' I commanded the blood vessels to be healed and the spirit of sickness to leave. I spent about ten minutes praying over her leg and foot. She didn't feel immediate evidence of healing, but the next morning her foot was warm. Later in the day, she told me her foot was cold again. I explained the nature of spiritual warfare and how the enemy tries to convince us we aren't healed. She smiled with understanding. I put my hands on her foot and commanded the symptoms to leave again and told her to do the same thing if the problem returned. Two weeks after I prayed over her foot, she posted a message on my Facebook page telling me her foot "still feels wonderful."

I learned a few things from these experiences. Healing is warfare on a level most of us can't fathom. There are no guarantees when it comes to healing. Someone you expect to be healed may die. Someone you don't expect to live may be healed. Life is full of uncertainties. You can shift the odds in your favor by cooperating with God.

CHAPTER EIGHTEEN

When Healing Doesn't Happen

SOMETIMES, THE ONE WE PRAY for will not be healed. Although supernatural healing is not an exact science, certain known issues exist that can prevent it or enhance it. In this chapter, I'll provide a list of the issues I've identified that may require troubleshooting, along with tips for better success. A brief description of each is provided with an explanation of how it can impact healing.

Issues That Prevent Healing

Inaccurate Identity: Authority is effectively exercised when we know our identity as beloved children of God in the depths of our spirit and soul. Faith for the miraculous is equivalent to confidence. Confidence comes from knowing our identity. If one's identity in Christ is not firmly established, one can expect inconsistent results.

Failure to Exercise Authority: The key to healing and removing demons is properly exercising authority. Authority is generally exercised through a command issued in faith. Anything that weakens faith hinders healing. Exercising authority requires practice.

Failure to Release Power: Creative miracles happen when the power of God that dwells in us is released through faith. One mentally believes they are releasing the power of God, and power is released. Fear and doubt hinder the release of power. Releasing power consistently requires practice.

Lack of Faith: The consistency with which we release power or exercise authority is determined by the condition of our faith. Weak faith, unbelief, fear, concern, worry, anxiety, and doubt lead to poor results. A mind filled with confidence and fearlessness produces consistent results. If your faith is lacking, find opportunities to practice the art of healing. Practice is the best way to increase faith. Ask God to allow you to operate in the gift of faith.

Evil Spirits: If a condition does not respond to the release of power and exercise of authority, consider whether an evil spirit must be removed. Many conditions, both physical and mental, are caused by evil spirits. When an evil spirit is present, an authoritative command must be issued for it to leave.

Unforgiveness: Some conditions, including chronic pain, are tied to unforgiveness. Sometimes, when using power and authority doesn't seem to work, consider whether there's anger or unforgiveness from the past that needs to be released to pave the way for healing.

Emotional Trauma: Many diseases and apparent physical illnesses are rooted in emotional trauma. Healing emotional wounds and removing demons can bring physical healing, where exercising authority and releasing power won't.

Accusations Not Addressed in the Court of Heaven: Some conditions will persist as long as an accusation in the court of heaven has not been addressed. For more information, check out my book *Defeating Your Adversary in the Court of Heaven.*

Curses: A curse—whether generational or some other type—can keep us trapped in sickness, poverty, and sin. Curses can be broken by issuing an authoritative declaration that the power of the curse be broken.

Verbal Agreements and Inner Vows: Similar to the way a curse works, we can make vows and agreements that empower sickness, poverty, and other conditions that thwart God's blessings. An authoritative command can break the power of ungodly agreements and inner vows. (Inner vows are discussed in a later chapter.)

Corrupted DNA: Some conditions are the result of DNA mutations. Ask the Holy Spirit for a strategy to heal damaged DNA.

Demonic Devices: Some conditions (particularly some forms of tinnitus) result from the existence of demonic devices in the spiritual realm like vices, knives, spears, and such. Ask the Holy Spirit to reveal a demonic device and ask for a strategy to remove it.

Being a Poor Receiver: Some people receive healing easily. Others have difficulty due to feelings of unworthiness, guilt, and fear of disappointment. The problem is how we view ourselves and God. The belief that God doesn't want to heal us can itself prevent us from receiving healing. It may be necessary to change our view of God or ourselves.

Stubbornness: When the Syrian King Naaman wanted to be healed of leprosy, the prophet Elisha told him to dip himself in the Jordan river seven times. Naaman was enraged. But a servant suggested that he swallow his pride and do as the prophet said. After dipping himself in the Jordan seven times, he was healed. God may have instructed you to do something you would rather not do. As long as you resist God's instruction, the condition will remain.

Poor Nutrition and Exercise: Nutrition and exercise play major roles in our health. For example, sugar is known to cause inflammation that leads to chronic pain. Some chronic pain syndromes can be cured by simply eliminating foods with processed sugar.

Damage to the Immune System: Our immune system fights infection, parasites, and invading organisms. Due to a variety of reasons, many people have damaged immune systems. Taking steps to repair your immune system will lead to improved health. Examples are taking vitamins and supplements such as zinc, vitamin C, and vitamin D.

Tips For Success

God's Presence: God's manifest presence by itself may bring healing, creative miracles, and deliverance from evil spirits. Ask God to bring His presence for whatever is needed. Many people can sense when they are in God's presence.

Word of Knowledge: God knows the reason why an illness remains despite prayer. Ask the Holy Spirit to reveal the problem and the solution.

An Attitude of Gratitude: I received a testimony from a man I had prayed with for healing of a frozen shoulder. His healing did not immediately manifest. Despite this, whenever he sensed pain or restricted range of motion, he thanked God for his healing. He did this several times a day. A couple of weeks after I prayed for him, he was at a basketball game. As he sat in the bleachers, a souvenir t-shirt was launched toward him. He reached up to catch it with his injured arm and realized it had been healed. He had no pain and he had regained normal range of motion. Sometimes, having the right attitude makes all the difference.

Pray More Than Once: Many times, when I pray for someone to be healed, it requires half a dozen attempts for the symptoms to resolve completely. If you pray once and nothing changes, pray again and ask the Holy Spirit for the best strategy.

Exercise

If you've prayed for someone, or possibly yourself, and you were unsuccessful, try to identify what issues may have been present that prevented the success of the prayer. Once you've identified the issue(s), try changing your approach or mindset as needed, and try praying again.

CHAPTER NINETEEN

Blessings and Curses

THE BIBLE SUGGESTS THAT OUR words have the power to affect others, for both good and bad. Words that have a positive effect on others (or ourselves) are referred to as *blessings*. Words that have a negative effect are called *curses*. During the creation of the earth and its inhabitants, God spoke a blessing over that which he had created:

> *Then God said, "Let the waters abound with an abundance of living creatures, and let birds fly above the earth across the face of the firmament of the heavens." So God created great sea creatures and every living thing that moves, with which the waters abounded, according to their kind, and every winged bird according to its kind. And God saw that it was good. And God blessed them, saying, "Be fruitful and multiply, and fill the waters in the seas, and let birds multiply on the earth."*
> GEN. 1:20-22

We don't know how many birds and fish were created, but the blessing of God empowered them to multiply. We might infer that had He not spoken such a blessing, their ability to multiply may have been diminished. A similar blessing was spoken over man:

> *Then God said, "Let Us make man in Our image, according to Our likeness; let them have dominion over the fish of the sea, over the birds of the air, and over the cattle, over all the earth and over every creeping thing that creeps on the earth." So God created man in His own image; in the image of God He created him; male and female He created them. Then God blessed them, and God said to them, "Be fruitful and multiply; fill the earth and subdue it; have dominion over the fish of the sea, over the birds of the air, and over every living thing that moves on the earth."*
> GEN. 1:26-28

In the same way that God blessed the birds and fish, He blessed man so that he would multiply. But the blessing upon man included the instruction to rule (have dominion) over all that had been created. God gave man the authority to rule over this newly created kingdom and that authority was bestowed through a blessing.

> *The patriarchs of Israel spoke blessings over their children that carried great significance. When he neared the end of his life, Isaac called his sons Jacob and Esau to his side to speak a blessing over them. Esau was the older brother and deserved the greater blessing. But Isaac's wife Rebekah put animal hair on Jacob's arms to make his father think he was Esau. She favored Jacob and wanted him to receive the blessing of the eldest son. This story is found in Genesis chapter 27:*
>
> *Isaac said to Jacob, "Please come near, that I may feel you, my son, whether you are really my son Esau or not." So Jacob went near to Isaac his father, and he felt him and said, "The voice is Jacob's voice, but the hands are the hands of Esau." And he did not recognize him, because his hands were hairy like his brother Esau's hands; so he blessed him.*
>
> *Then he said, "Are you really my son Esau?"*

He said, "I am."

He said, "Bring it near to me, and I will eat of my son's game, so that my soul may bless you." So he brought it near to him, and he ate; and he brought him wine, and he drank. Then his father Isaac said to him, "Come near now and kiss me, my son." And he came near and kissed him; and he smelled the smell of his clothing, and blessed him and said:

"Surely, the smell of my son
Is like the smell of a field
Which the Lord has blessed.
Therefore may God give you
Of the dew of heaven,
Of the fatness of the earth,
And plenty of grain and wine.
Let peoples serve you,
And nations bow down to you.
Be master over your brethren,
And let your mother's sons bow down to you.
Cursed be everyone who curses you,
And blessed be those who bless you!"

Now it happened, as soon as Isaac had finished blessing Jacob, and Jacob had scarcely gone out from the presence of Isaac his father, that Esau his brother came in from his hunting. He also had made savory food, and brought it to his father, and said to his father, "Let my father arise and eat of his son's game, that your soul may bless me."

And his father Isaac said to him, "Who are you?"

So he said, "I am your son, your firstborn, Esau."

Then Isaac trembled exceedingly, and said, "Who? Where is the one who hunted game and brought it to me? I ate all of it before you came, and I have blessed him—and indeed he shall be blessed."

When Esau heard the words of his father, he cried with an exceed-

ingly great and bitter cry, and said to his father, "Bless me—me also, O my father!"

But he said, "Your brother came with deceit and has taken away your blessing."

And Esau said, "Is he not rightly named Jacob? For he has supplanted me these two times. He took away my birthright, and now look, he has taken away my blessing!" And he said, "Have you not reserved a blessing for me?"

Then Isaac answered and said to Esau, "Indeed I have made him your master, and all his brethren I have given to him as servants; with grain and wine I have sustained him. What shall I do now for you, my son?"

And Esau said to his father, "Have you only one blessing, my father? Bless me—me also, O my father!" And Esau lifted up his voice and wept.
GEN. 27:21-38

The Bible is full of stories of how blessings and curses were spoken that affected those under their influence. This verse from the book of Proverbs suggests that our words are capable of bringing life or death:

Death and life are in the power of the tongue, And those who love it will eat its fruit.
PROV. 18:21

Some may wonder how one's words can change the destiny of another. The kingdom of heaven and the kingdom of darkness exist in the spiritual world. One cannot experience them through the senses of the physical body. The spiritual dimension is experienced by our spirit. Spirit beings like God and Satan do not usually exert direct control over the physical world. Instead, they accomplish their will by exerting influence over humans. Whether knowingly or unknowingly, we carry out their will in the earth. Some of us cooperate with the Holy Spirit and angels. Others submit to the influence of demons. The Holy Spirit guides our spirit in an attempt to bring our thoughts, words, and actions into alignment with heaven's agenda. As heaven's representatives, we can speak a blessing over someone that is in accordance with God's will. Such a blessing carries spiritual authority, as we were given such authority through Jesus. Non-believers may speak blessings as well, but they do not carry the same God-given authority. When a believer speaks a blessing, angels and the Holy Spirit attempt to influence other humans to make the blessing come to pass.

The dynamic of blessing others is illustrated in the story of Balaam, the prophet who was recruited by Balak, the King of Moab to curse the Israelites. Although Balaam initially agreed to curse God's people, an angel warned the prophet not to say anything except that which the Lord had authorized. Rather than cursing God's people, Balaam spoke a blessing:

Then the Lord met Balaam, and put a word in his mouth, and said, "Go back to Balak, and thus you shall speak." So he came to him, and there he was, standing by his burnt offering, and the princes of Moab were with him. And Balak said to him, "What has the Lord spoken?"

Then he took up his oracle and said:

"Rise up, Balak, and hear!
Listen to me, son of Zippor!

God is not a man, that He should lie,
Nor a son of man, that He should repent.
Has He said, and will He not do?
Or has He spoken, and will He not make it good?
Behold, I have received a command to bless;
He has blessed, and I cannot reverse it.

He has not observed iniquity in Jacob,
Nor has He seen wickedness in Israel.
The Lord his God is with him,
And the shout of a King is among them.
God brings them out of Egypt;
He has strength like a wild ox.

117

For there is no sorcery against Jacob,
Nor any divination against Israel.
It now must be said of Jacob
And of Israel, 'Oh, what God has done!'
Look, a people rises like a lioness,
And lifts itself up like a lion;
It shall not lie down until it devours the prey,
And drinks the blood of the slain."

Then Balak said to Balaam, "Neither curse them at all, nor bless them at all!"

So Balaam answered and said to Balak, "Did I not tell you, saying, 'All that the Lord speaks, that I must do?'"
NUM. 23:16-26

Balaam could have cursed God's people. But instead, he exercised his free will and chose to bless them. In doing so, he helped bring to pass God's will.

The same principle also applies to curses. Demons attempt to influence us to bring our thoughts, words, and actions into alignment with Satan's agenda. When a curse is spoken, spiritual beings such as demons attempt to influence other humans to bring it to fruition. This principle was demonstrated when God spoke a curse over Adam's son Cain after he murdered his brother Abel. The account is found in the book of Genesis:

Now Cain talked with Abel his brother; and it came to pass, when they were in the field, that Cain rose up against Abel his brother and killed him.

Then the Lord said to Cain, "Where is Abel your brother?"

He said, "I do not know. Am I my brother's keeper?"

And He said, "What have you done? The voice of your brother's blood cries out to Me from the ground. So now you are cursed from the earth, which has opened its mouth to receive your brother's blood from your hand. When you till the ground, it shall no longer yield its strength to you. A fugitive and a vagabond you shall be on the earth."

And Cain said to the Lord, "My punishment is greater than I can bear! Surely You have driven me out this day from the face of the ground; I shall be hidden from Your face; I shall be a fugitive and a vagabond on the earth, and it will happen that anyone who finds me will kill me."

And the Lord said to him, "Therefore, whoever kills Cain, vengeance shall be taken on him sevenfold." And the Lord set a mark on Cain, lest anyone finding him should kill him.
GEN. 4:8-15

The curse God spoke over Cain came with a mark so that others would know he was cursed. The mark apparently contained instructions about the nature of the curse so that anyone who met him could take the appropriate action. The same principle may apply to all blessings and curses. When one speaks a blessing or curse over another, it may leave a spiritual mark on them with instructions to angels and demons about the actions they should take.

The kingdom of God and the kingdom of darkness appear to use different mechanisms to enforce their blessings and curses. These mechanisms were illustrated by Jesus. After He chose His 12 disciples and gave them power and authority to heal and remove demons, He commissioned 70 more and told them to do likewise. In Luke chapter 10, we find the report of the 70 upon their return. (This passage is from the King James version):

And the seventy returned again with joy, saying, Lord, even the devils are subject unto us through thy name. And he said unto them, I beheld Satan as lightning fall from heaven. Behold, I give unto you power to tread on serpents and scorpions, and over all the power of the enemy: and nothing shall by any means hurt you. Notwithstanding in this rejoice not, that the spirits are subject unto you; but rather rejoice, because your names are written in heaven."
LUKE 10:17-20 KJV

There is a mistranslation in this passage. Verse 19 reads: "I give unto you power to tread on serpents and scorpions, and over all the power of the enemy." In the Greek New Testament, the second occurrence of the word power is "dunamis," and it is correctly translated. But the first occurrence of the word is "exousia," which should be translated "authority." The New King James correctly translates this verse: "Behold, I give you the *authority* to trample on serpents and scorpions, and over all the *power* of the enemy, and nothing shall by any means hurt you." Jesus explained why demons were subject to the disciples: The authority they had received was greater than the enemy's power. Note that He compared two different concepts: authority and power.

Why did He not say that the disciples' authority was greater than the authority of the enemy? Because authority is granted to one being from another who has authority. God is the ultimate authority in the universe and He has granted Satan no legitimate authority. In verse 18 of this passage, the Lord said He saw Satan fall like lightning from heaven. The implication is that Satan once had authority, but he abused it, so it was removed. Any claim he makes to have authority is fraudulent.

Although Satan has no legitimate authority, he is permitted to use power. Indeed, the kingdom of darkness accomplishes its objectives through the use of power or energy. But the authority we receive from God is greater than the power used by the enemy. When we find ourselves cursed by someone who used the power of darkness, we can exercise authority and neutralize it.

In 2022, I created a series of videos where I prayed for various conditions to be healed. I've received hundreds of healing testimonies from people who have listened to them. What follows is a testimony from a woman who was rescued from what she referred to as the curse of death while listening to one of the videos:

> A few weeks after your first healing video and reading numerous testimonials on your telegram channel, I decided to watch it myself. During the healing session, I was following your advice and relaxing with my eyes closed. I felt tingling in my brain during some of the session, but the instant you said, "I break all curses," I saw a vision of the moment a death curse was placed over me. It happened while I was 21 years old (I'm 37 now) while working in the mall. I was a manager in foods and my boss had asked

me how an older woman was working out in the store. I gave him my honest thoughts (she's sweet but she physically cannot do the job). He ended up letting her go, at which point she came to seek me out, and began to tell me how much she hated me and prayed every day that I would die and go to hell. I was devastated that day, but hadn't thought of that moment in years. As I watched it replay, I had the strong impression of God saying "this was a death curse on you and I'm breaking it." I then saw the moment both shatter as glass and tear like paper. It was a lot happening in a second, because I kept hearing every word you said, but it was like everything paused while this vision played out. The instant this curse was broken, I also "knew" God was also showing me that I could trust you and that He was with you. So, I do.

I didn't know that it was a curse until God told me. The year that the woman cursed me was the year I began to slowly spiral down, and a divide felt in place between God and me. I fell into a sexual addiction sin shortly after that. I always knew something was keeping me from the deep walk with Christ that I had always had, but I couldn't pinpoint anything. I always knew that God was there, and I was not giving up, but it was like being blind, trying to find Him in a house I'd never been in. Probably months before finding you, the Spirit led me to cast out the demon causing the addiction, and I continued my fighting climb up again to the Lord; everything was reversing. The curse-breaking was one of the last pieces to fall into place.

The woman who fell under the power of the curse experienced a sudden, unexplained feeling as if she was separated from God. She also fell into sexual addiction. Whenever we experience a sudden change in mood, behavior, or sensation, or an ungodly desire takes hold of us, we may have come under the power of a curse or spell. Headaches, dizziness, disorientation, ringing in the ears, nausea, and vomiting are common physical manifestations of a curse. Feeling as if we are separated from God, depression, anxiety, fear, panic attacks, helplessness, and lethargy are emotional manifestations. A sudden uncontrollable desire for sex, alcohol, or illicit substances are other signs of a curse.

The effect of a curse is the same whether one knowingly operates in dark practices like witchcraft or merely speaks a curse out of anger. Because God wants to bless others through us, Jesus instructed His disciples to love their enemies and pray for them rather than cursing them:

"You have heard that it was said, 'You shall love your neighbor and hate your enemy.' But I say to you, love your enemies, bless

those who curse you, do good to those who hate you, and pray for those who spitefully use you and persecute you, that you may be sons of your Father in heaven; for He makes His sun rise on the evil and on the good, and sends rain on the just and on the unjust."
MATT. 5:43-45

It can be a challenge praying sincerely for one's enemies. It is even more difficult to speak a blessing over them. But if we do not, we empower the work of Satan. God wants to bestow His blessings upon all, the just and the unjust. But if we do not speak His blessings over others and instead curse them, rather than using our authority to establish His will, Satan will use our words to bring death and destruction.

There are many types of curses. Most of them can be neutralized in the same way. An authoritative command should be made stating that the power of a curse is broken. When an authoritative command is issued in faith, authority is exercised, and the power of the enemy is vanquished.

The Bible suggests that a curse will not affect us unless we've done something to empower it:

Like a fluttering sparrow or a darting swallow, an undeserved curse will not land on its intended victim.
PROV. 26:2

In an earlier chapter, I described the time a demon overpowered me. That night, I asked God to put my wife's afflictions on me if it would help her condition. In saying these words, I opened the door for a demon to attack me. In essence, I spoke a curse over myself and came into agreement with the enemy's plan. After the demon was removed, I renounced the words I had said. My renunciation was a display of my changed intention. Instead of allowing my will to empower a curse, I aligned my intention with the will of God, which destroyed the power of the curse.

It's not unusual for someone to say they will never be successful, never be married, never speak in public, never be healed, or never find the right job. These (and similar) statements can act as curses. The enemy can use our own words against us to keep us from fulfilling our destiny or prevent us from being healed. My advice is to refrain from speaking such negative words into your life or that of another.

If you've come under the power of a curse—whether knowingly or unwittingly—you may need to renounce the words you've said or actions you've taken that have empowered it. You can renounce the agreement verbally and decree that the power of the curse is broken. This principle applies both to words you have said and words that are spoken by others.

Generational curses are a controversial matter. Some say these curses can affect families for generations, while others say they are a myth. If you believe (or if the Holy Spirit has indicated) that you or your family are under the power of a generational curse, you can break its power with an authoritative command. If you know of some action taken by an ancestor or a belief system they embraced that empowered the curse, you can renounce the activity or denounce the belief system. The Holy Spirit may give you specific words to say or actions to take.

CHAPTER TWENTY

Authority Over Weather

WHILE AUTHORITY IN THE CONTEXT of healing is widely accepted, the acknowledgment that God has given us authority over the weather is less common. Like many people, I was skeptical when this idea was first suggested to me, even though Jesus modeled such authority:

On the same day, when evening had come, He said to them, "Let us cross over to the other side." Now when they had left the multitude, they took Him along in the boat as He was. And other little boats were also with Him. And a great windstorm arose, and the waves beat into the boat, so that it was already filling. But He was in the stern, asleep on a pillow. And they awoke Him and said to Him, "Teacher, do You not care that we are perishing?"

Then He arose and rebuked the wind, and said to the sea, "Peace, be still!" And the wind ceased and there was a great calm. But

He said to them, "Why are you so fearful? How is it that you have
no faith?" And they feared exceedingly, and said to one another,
"Who can this be, that even the wind and the sea obey Him!"
MARK 4:35-41

Just as Jesus viewed sickness as something to be defeated, He saw
a storm on the Sea of Galilee as an opposing force. He rebuked the
fever that afflicted Peter's mother-in-law and made it vanish. In like
manner, He rebuked the storm, and it fled from His presence. Note
that He asked why the disciples were fearful. If they had acted in faith
instead of fear, might they have been able to calm the storm?

Jesus said His followers would do the same works that He did and
even greater ones:

"Most assuredly, I say to you, he who believes in Me, the works
that I do he will do also; and greater works than these he will do,
because I go to My Father."
JOHN 14:12

The word "disciple" means *student*. If you are a disciple of Jesus, you
are His student. His goal is to teach you to do the things He does. The
exercise of our authority is not limited to healing and making demons
homeless. Why wouldn't it extend to all areas of life and include changing the weather?

In September 2009, Denise and I attended the Spiritual Hunger Conference in Spokane, Washington. The conference proved to be a time of
great spiritual growth. God encouraged us to try things we had never
previously considered.

Before driving to the conference, I received an e-mail from my brother
who lives in Tennessee. That week, there had been severe flooding in
the southeast part of the United States. Atlanta, Georgia, had received
21 inches of rainfall in just a couple of days. My brother suggested that
I ask God to stop the rain.

Denise and I arrived at our hotel room in Spokane on a Thursday evening. As I left the hotel Friday morning for the conference, I walked

through the lobby and heard the weather forecaster on the television discussing the flooding in the southeast. Then I heard a voice in my mind say, "Why don't you do something about it?"

I was shocked to hear these words from what I knew to be the voice of the Holy Spirit. I quietly replied, "What do you mean 'why don't *I* do something about it?' I'm not God; you are. Why don't *you* do something about it?"

Walking through the hotel lobby the following day, I heard the weather forecaster report on the continued flooding. Again, I heard God say, "Why don't you do something about it?"

Once more, I quietly replied, "How am I supposed to stop a storm thousands of miles away? If you want to stop that storm, why don't you do something about it?"

I didn't believe in this sort of thing at the time. But I met some new friends named Robert and Gwendolyn and asked for their thoughts on the matter. Robert shared a testimony. "One time, we were going to the coast, and the forecast was for cloudy weather with highs in the 50s. I didn't want that. I wanted sunny weather with highs in the 60s, so I made some declarations to that effect, and when we got to the coast, it was sunny, and it stayed sunny the entire time we were there." Then Gwendolyn added a few of her own stories about commanding the weather to change. She believed we had the authority to do anything Jesus did. I knew the Holy Spirit was encouraging me to step out in faith and try something new, so we decided to go for it.

Later that day, I stood with my friends on the conference center lawn and we put our plan into action. Directing my voice to the sky, I spoke: "I command the storm in the southeast United States to move, in Jesus' name. I command the winds of change to move the low-pressure system out to sea over the Atlantic Ocean, in Jesus' name. Atmosphere, obey the voice of the children of God!" Gwendolyn, Robert, and my wife stood beside me on the lawn, making similar declarations.

I'm sure we looked a little nutty demanding that a storm should cease while standing under a clear blue sky in Spokane, but I didn't care.

I came to the realization that it didn't matter what strangers thought of me. I wanted to do what God asked me to do.

Excited to see if our declarations and commands worked, we gathered around the television Sunday morning in the lobby to check the weather. As the radar loop played, we could plainly see that the storm, which had been stalled for weeks over the southeast, had moved out to sea. Sunday's forecast was for plenty of sunshine.

Since then, I've commanded the weather to change whenever it seemed like property damage might occur. During the third week of July 2022, our city experienced severe thunderstorms nearly every night. Denise and I developed a habit of watching them on a radar tracker. One night, a severe thunderstorm began moving toward our neighborhood. We spoke to the storm when it was still a couple of hours away. We forbid it to bring damaging winds or heavy rain into our neighborhood. Just as the storm reached our location, it lost its intensity and dissipated. All we received was a sprinkle of light rain. A few miles away, the storm had caused extensive property damage. Since then, we've watched storms approach on radar, commanded them not to harm our neighborhood, and saw them split into two smaller storms—one going to the north and the other to the south of us.

The Arizona desert is famous for its dust storms that leave a fine layer of dirt over everything. In October of 2022, radar showed a large storm moving toward us from New Mexico. That afternoon, as it came closer, I occasionally told the storm it was not permitted to bring dirt onto our property. An hour before sunset, I looked toward the horizon and saw a wall of dust about five hundred feet high moving toward us. As it advanced, I continued commanding the storm not to bring dirt on our property. (The dirt from a single storm can take days to clean up, and the winds that carry the dust can uproot trees.) The wall of dust was now within half a mile of our home, and it obscured the sun. Although our property was surrounded by swirling dust in every direction, when I went outside after the storm had passed, there was no sign of dirt anywhere on our property. The storm had obeyed my commands.

A few common-sense principles should be applied when exercising authority over weather. There may be times when we should exercise authority and times when we should not. Jesus calmed a storm that had the potential to kill Him and the disciples. When lives are at risk, we should use our authority to prevent death or injury. Tornadoes, strong hurricanes, and thunderstorms that could kill people seem to be fair game. But we should not rebuke every storm simply because we can. The area where I live only receives about ten inches of rain a year. I don't want to command every thunderstorm to cease. Doing so would cause a drought, which could lead to crop death.

Although prophets of the Old Testament operated in this kind of authority, I would not advise speaking a drought into existence without direct instruction from God and, perhaps, independent confirmation from spiritually mature individuals. It is equally within our authority to command rain to fall, if we're experiencing a drought.

Generally, when I speak to a storm, I set boundaries. Rain is permitted, but not excessive precipitation that leads to flooding. Winds are allowed as long as they are gentle and don't cause property damage or loss of life. I don't feel it's necessary to set ideal conditions for every weather system; my goal is to limit property damage and loss of life.

Commanding the weather to obey us is not the stuff of Sunday sermons. But it is a perfectly biblical way to represent God and His kingdom. The Holy Spirit can give personal guidelines for operating in this kind of authority if you ask Him.

CHAPTER TWENTY-ONE

Multiplication of Food

THE AREAS OF LIFE OVER which we may exercise authority are practically without limit. In the following chapters, we'll examine a few controversial ones.

Up to this point, it has been a straightforward process identifying whether an issue should be addressed by releasing power or exercising authority. Generally speaking, exercising authority removes things that should not be present. A release of power creates things that are missing or repairs things that are damaged. The issues we're about to explore do not lend themselves to such clearcut explanations. In some cases, an argument could be made for either power or authority. And in others, God sovereignly works a miracle simply to bless us.

Moses led the Israelites into the wilderness for 40 years rather than into the promised land. The detour was necessary because the people had become fearful and thought God could not give them victory over the Canaanites who inhabited the land God promised. Despite their unbelief, God used their wanderings in the wilderness to show them His ability to care for all their needs. Exodus chapter 16 contains a fascinating promise from God:

Then the Lord said to Moses, "Behold, I will rain bread from heaven for you. And the people shall go out and gather a certain quota every day, that I may test them, whether they will walk in My law or not. And it shall be on the sixth day that they shall prepare what they bring in, and it shall be twice as much as they gather daily."
EX. 16:4-5

In Deuteronomy chapter 29, Moses recounted the ways in which God provided for His people while they lived in the wilderness. In verse five we learn that the Lord not only fed them manna from heaven but made sure their clothing did not wear out:

And I have led you forty years in the wilderness. Your clothes have not worn out on you, and your sandals have not worn out on your feet.

God supernaturally met the needs of His people because He loves them and desires to bless them. Jesus illustrated that same principle. The wedding in Cana provided the opportunity for Him to work His first miracle:

On the third day there was a wedding in Cana of Galilee, and the mother of Jesus was there. Now both Jesus and His disciples were invited to the wedding. And when they ran out of wine, the mother of Jesus said to Him, "They have no wine."

Jesus said to her, "Woman, what does your concern have to do with Me? My hour has not yet come."

His mother said to the servants, "Whatever He says to you, do it."

Now there were set there six waterpots of stone, according to the manner of purification of the Jews, containing twenty or thirty

gallons apiece. Jesus said to them, "Fill the waterpots with water."
And they filled them up to the brim. And He said to them, "Draw
some out now, and take it to the master of the feast." And they
took it. When the master of the feast had tasted the water that
was made wine, and did not know where it came from (but the
servants who had drawn the water knew), the master of the feast
called the bridegroom. And he said to him, "Every man at the
beginning sets out the good wine, and when the guests have well
drunk, then the inferior. You have kept the good wine until now!"

This beginning of signs Jesus did in Cana of Galilee, and mani-
fested His glory; and His disciples believed in Him.
JOHN 2:1-11

When the wedding party ran out of wine, Mary, the mother of Jesus,
came to Him for help. His reply suggested there was nothing He could
do because His time to work miracles had not yet arrived. But a few
minutes later, apparently, it had. And water was turned into wine.

It isn't clear whether the transformation of water into wine happened due
to the release of power or the exercise of authority. One might think that
because the wine was created miraculously from another substance, it
involved the release of power since the release of power works creative
miracles. But one could argue that Jesus exercised authority.

When the ten lepers were healed, it was due to an exercise of authority.
Jesus issued an authoritative command for them to show themselves
to the priests. Because they believed He could heal them, they obeyed
His command and were healed.

In the same way, the Lord instructed the servants to fill a few empty
pots with water, draw some out and take it to the master of the feast.
This must have been an uncomfortable predicament for the servants.
Jesus told them to take what they believed to be water to the master.
This would lead to great embarrassment because the wedding party
would expect wine. But Mary tipped off the servants when she said,
"Whatever He says to you, do it." She seemed to know that Jesus would
solve the problem even if she did not know how or when. The servants
apparently believed something would happen to change the expected

outcome. They obeyed the command of Jesus and filled a container with water, took it to the master, and it became wine.

I don't think we need to take a firm stand on whether it happened due to the exercise of authority or the release of power. I only want to point out that it is not always clear which mechanism is used. The same principle applies to the next miracle we'll examine.

It is usually taught that Jesus multiplied a few loaves of bread and a couple of fish to feed thousands of people, but is that true?

Let's look at the account from Mark's gospel:

> *When the day was now far spent, His disciples came to Him and said, "This is a deserted place, and already the hour is late. Send them away, that they may go into the surrounding country and villages and buy themselves bread; for they have nothing to eat."*
>
> *But He answered and said to them, "You give them something to eat."*
>
> *And they said to Him, "Shall we go and buy two hundred denarii worth of bread and give them something to eat?"*
>
> *But He said to them, "How many loaves do you have? Go and see."*
>
> *And when they found out they said, "Five, and two fish."*
>
> *Then He commanded them to make them all sit down in groups on the green grass. So, they sat down in ranks, in hundreds and in fifties. And when He had taken the five loaves and the two fish, He looked up to heaven, blessed and broke the loaves, and gave them to His disciples to set before them; and the two fish He divided among them all. So, they all ate and were filled. And they took up twelve baskets full of fragments and of the fish. Now those who had eaten the loaves were about five thousand men.*
> MARK 6:35-44

When the disciples perceived that the people were hungry, their solution was to send them away to find food for themselves. However, Jesus had a different plan. He did not suggest that *He* would feed the multitude Himself; He told *the disciples* to feed them. The disciples were naturally perplexed and complained that such a feat was impossible.

Jesus took what food they had—five loaves of bread and two fish—and blessed them. He divided the two fish into pieces and then handed to the disciples the same quantity of food He had received from them. The food had not yet multiplied. It would have been impractical to hand back enough food to feed thousands of people. Instead, he instructed them to distribute the not-yet-multiplied food to the multitude. As they passed it out, it multiplied in their hands. Because the food had not yet multiplied when Jesus handed it back, the disciples had to *believe* that, somehow, there would be enough to feed thousands of people. Their *faith* and *obedience* caused the food to multiply in their hands.

Did the food multiply due to power being released, or was it an exercise of authority? An argument can be made for both possibilities. Power could have been released to create more food. Or, the authoritative command, when followed faithfully by the disciples, may have caused the food to multiply.

You may be surprised to learn that miracles of multiplication are still happening today. In December 2022, I received the following testimony:

> I had a miracle happen over Thanksgiving. As I was making some food, namely dessert for my extended family, I realized I should have gotten a third tub of whipped cream. But I was going to just make the two I bought go as far as I could. I used one tub the day before and was going to finish up the next day. When I went to the fridge to finish it the next day, there were still two tubs in the fridge, both sealed! I just stopped and thanked God with tears in my eyes. He didn't have to do that, but I know He's showing what He'll do for those who trust in Him as our provider! Not only that, but He's providing for more than just our needs (no one needs dessert, lol)!

Here's another testimony that I received in the fall of 2022:

> Hi, Praying Medic,
>
> I just wanted to share the awesomeness of God! The other day, I asked God to please multiply our food. I was mainly thinking about our three boys. Well, these chicken

tender things appeared in our freezer, front and center. I thought my husband had bought them. I haven't bought these specific tenders in years.

Tonight, when looking for something to eat, I pulled them out. I asked my husband, and he said he didn't buy them. He even called his mom because we both thought maybe there was a chance that she sent some home with our boys. Nope. And no one has been in our house. I totally remembered that I had asked God to multiply our food! My husband thought there might be a chance they could have been old and expired, but the expiration date was in 2023!

I told my husband and our children that God provided us with dinner. And guess what it was? "HONEY" chicken tenders! Is that not symbolic/prophetic, or what! He is so cool.

I've received dozens of testimonies from grateful people who have witnessed God multiply many different things. One woman sent me the following testimony:

We just had our floors re-done. The night before they were to finish, they said they were going to need three more boxes of the flooring we were putting in. They said they would finish what we had and come back to finish when the flooring came in. These were special order planks, and it would take three weeks to get them in. I asked God to multiply the planks we needed to finish the floors. Not only did he provide enough flooring to finish the floors, but they had four planks left over! The installers were shocked; I said God answers prayers, and he said, "Yes, he does."

Thanks be to God, and thank you for your teaching.

Another woman sent me this testimony:

On June 22nd, I experienced a surprising miracle. I noticed my gas tank was on empty as I drove to my son's house to take care of my granddaughter that morning. I didn't want to be late, because my daughter-in-law had an appointment. I had enough gas to get to their house, so I decided I would refuel at a station nearby before returning home. However, by the time I left their house five hours later, all I could think of was getting home and crawling in bed to rest. Narry a thought about being on empty. After a long nap, I got up to go to the grocery store. A block from my home, I happened to glance at the gas gauge. I remembered the empty light, just as I noticed that the gauge showed completely full! Absolutely stunned, I immediately pulled over to the curb to absorb the reality of what had happened to me. I never asked for this or even thought to ask God for gas. What unusual kindness! For years I have been running on empty. I felt He was saying that He was going to fill my tank with energy. I don't know how it will all play out, but I am overwhelmed by His love and goodness! Thank you for your part in what God is doing in my life!

Finally, I received this testimony:

Our BBQ gas bottle has not run out since before last Christmas. Five full months of weekly use, and it is still pumping out that gas. Definitely unusual. It felt so light we were sure it was about to run out, and that was two months ago. So, each Friday night (BBQ night), we give thanks, and still smile in amazement.

I LOVE what God is doing!

I know people who see a recipe make twice as many biscuits or muffins as it should. Many people have seen God fill their gas tanks after prayer. Others chose to command their gas tank to remain full. I know people who pray over their pantries, and their food lasts much longer than it should. A friend prayed over a dry well on his property, and not long afterward, it produced clean, drinkable water. The ways in which God wants to bless us are innumerable. If you're willing to think outside the bounds of what is considered normal and, in faith, believe that He will do the unexpected, you will see His goodness manifest in your life.

CHAPTER TWENTY-TWO

Supernatural Repair of Electronic Devices

JUST AS JESUS GIVES US authority to heal the sick and command storms to cease, we have authority to heal broken electronic devices, appliances, cars, and other machines. Because electronic devices and modern machines did not exist when the Bible was written, this chapter will rely on personal testimonies.

Years ago, my wife was given a Bose iPod docking station from her son as a gift. The docking station is a portable sound system that amplifies an Apple iPod. Bose makes some of the best sound equipment available, and the docking station got a lot of use. In the summer, we would put it out by our pool to have music outside. At the time, it was our only device for listening to music, except our computers.

One day, the docking station gave up the ghost. It suddenly stopped working. We tried plugging it into different outlets, checked for loose

POWER AND AUTHORITY MADE SIMPLE

connections, and did the usual troubleshooting to no avail. Her beloved iPod dock was toast.

Our friend Gwendolyn and her husband Larry had been in our area for a couple of weeks. So, we invited them over and planned a dinner party beside the pool.

Gwen's life with Jesus is a little unusual. She taught me how to command storms to cease. She drives her car for days on an empty gas tank. She has incredible faith in God and knows how to exercise authority.

When they arrived, we were preparing for the evening. Denise took the broken docking station outside and placed it on a table, knowing it did not work. I didn't think much about it at the time.

We made some margaritas and got comfortable on the patio. After a few minutes of conversation, Gwen and Denise decided it was time to pray over the broken iPod dock so that we could have music. (I later learned that Denise had this entire process planned out.) She believed that if, by faith, she brought it outside, plugged it in, and had us pray over it, it would be repaired.

So, that's what we did.

The four of us stood in agreement and declared the docking station would be repaired. While I was praying, I saw a vision of broken electrical wires, so I commanded them to be made new. The others prayed as they were led by the Spirit. After praying, Denise confidently turned the iPod on. Music came forth. The docking station worked flawlessly after that day.

I can't recommend a specific prayer for the supernatural repair of electronic devices. Many people have shared similar testimonies with me. In each case, the approach used was unique. As is true for most types of prayer, the most effective method is praying in whatever way the Holy Spirit leads. Here is another testimony.

When I feel inspired to write, I try to make the most of the opportunity, which is why I'm rarely without my laptop computer. When I worked as a paramedic, I could usually be found pecking away at an article or the chapter of my next book when I wasn't on a call. A few years ago, I pulled my trusty laptop computer from its case, plugged it into a wall outlet in a hospital waiting room, and turned on the power switch.

Nothing happened.

The green and red diodes on the front panel remained dark. It took my mind about five-hundredths of a second to process the most likely explanations—and for a moment, I was overcome with panic. Don't panic, I thought to myself. Maybe the outlet isn't working. I unplugged the power cord from the wall and plugged it into another outlet nearby.

Nothing happened.

I went to a different room and tried plugging it into several outlets, but still, there were no illuminated lights on the panel. The computer would not turn on. My desperation grew, but I had one more thought. Maybe the power cord was bad. I went to my ambulance and found the power cord for the computer we used to chart calls. It uses the same voltage as my computer. It was connected to our work laptop, and it was working normally. I removed the plug from that computer and plugged it into mine.

Nothing.

So, it wasn't a lack of power, and it wasn't a bad cord. There was some internal problem with my laptop that prevented it from powering up. The panic returned. My laptop is a Panasonic Toughbook. These computers are used by the military, law enforcement, and EMS because they're nearly indestructible. I've had mine for over ten years, and although it's suffered its share of abuse, it never failed me. It's the best laptop I've ever owned. And now it was deader than dead. I was in the middle of writing a book, and the hassle of buying a replacement computer and transferring the files was not something I looked forward to.

Then another thought came to me. Why don't you pray for it to be resurrected? Yes, I thought, that's the ticket! I need to pray for it. But first, I needed breakfast and a cup of coffee.

I left the laptop in the ambulance and went inside the hospital. I went to the cafeteria, ordered a breakfast sandwich and a cup of coffee, and then sat at a table. I recalled some of the dead electronic devices and broken cars I'd seen God heal over the years when we prayed over them. As I thought about these testimonies and the awesomeness of God, my sense of panic was replaced by faith. God had done it before; why wouldn't He do it again?

I finished my sandwich and walked back to the ambulance with my cup of coffee. I opened the side door of the ambulance and placed the dead computer on the floor. I placed my hand on it and made declarations. "This computer will live and not die. It will be resurrected from the dead, and it will work as it is supposed to." I felt even more faith as I prayed. After a couple of minutes, I felt confident it would now power up. I plugged the laptop's power cord into the outlet in the ambulance, and the red diode for the battery charge indicator immediately came on. I hit the power switch. The hard drive hummed. The diodes sprang to life. My beloved laptop had been raised from the dead. I took it back to the waiting room and plugged it in. It charged without problems off the same wall outlet I had tried without success 30 minutes earlier.

When my computer failed to power up, I could have resigned myself to the idea that it was time to replace it. That is what most people would do. But the kingdom of God is one of limitless possibilities. I did not know with certainty if I could bring a computer back to life, but I felt it was worth a try. You might feel silly praying over a broken car, refrigerator or washing machine, and an uninformed observer might ridicule you. Fear of what others think can prevent us from operating in the supernatural. But when faith activates authority, anything is possible.

I frequently receive testimonies from people who have seen appliances, air conditioners, toilets, broken cars, and other objects supernaturally repaired. God cares about the things that matter to you. The authority He's given you has application in areas you've never dreamed of. I would encourage you to step out in faith and believe for a miracle whenever the need arises.

CHAPTER TWENTY-THREE

Modes of Prayer

GOD HAS MADE AVAILABLE TO us a variety of techniques that are collectively called *prayer*. This chapter will explore how we communicate with our Creator, pray for others, and exercise authority.

I'm often asked: Why does it seem as if God doesn't hear my prayers?

Many of us have been taught that prayer equals asking God for something we need or want. If we receive what we ask for, this is equivalent to God hearing and answering our prayer. In this dynamic, communication with God is little more than asking for something and receiving it. If we receive something, we are told that God hears our prayers. If not, we assume He does not hear our prayers.

This idea may be fine for little children, but it is not how mature believers communicate with God. We know God is a Spirit. He communicates with us using spiritual language. His voice may be detected through the faint thought impressions that some refer to as the "still, small voice." He also speaks through visions, dreams, and on rare occasions, through what appears to be an audible voice. Rather than merely listening for God's answer to our prayer as a change in circumstance, we should also listen for His voice speaking to our spirit.

The Bible says that God knows the thoughts and intentions of our hearts. He hears our thoughts and speaks to us through thought impressions. Strictly speaking, it isn't necessary to use our voice to communicate with Him. Whatever thoughts come to our mind, He hears them just as clearly as we do. Communication with God is done heart to heart, spirit to spirit. This is not to say that we *cannot* speak audibly to God. I often do. But it is to say that words are not *necessary*. Speaking to others audibly is a common form of human communication that feels natural and complete. But with God, it is optional.

As my relationship with God has grown, I've developed a daily habit of—sometimes constant—communication with Him that could be described as small talk. In the same way that I engage in conversations with my wife about mundane topics such as what to eat, I routinely communicate with God about trivial matters. This kind of prayer is not spoken. It is the conveyance of thoughts from one being to another. Very little of our conversation has to do with the requests I make to Him. Whether I receive what I ask for is not an indicator of whether He hears me. I know He hears me because He is always responding to my thoughts toward Him.

Prayer

When Jesus engaged in what the Bible refers to as "prayer," He often did it in solitude:

> *Now it came to pass in those days that He went out to the mountain to pray, and continued all night in prayer to God. And when it was day, He called His disciples to Himself; and from them He chose twelve whom He also named apostles.*
> LUKE 6:12-13

I don't know what I would have seen or heard had I witnessed Jesus praying to His Father. But when I pray to Him, it's usually an informal discussion. My conversations with God are a continual dialogue without a clearly defined beginning or end. This may be what the Apostle Paul meant when he encouraged believers to pray without ceasing:

> *Rejoice always, pray without ceasing, in everything give thanks; for this is the will of God in Christ Jesus for you.*
> 1 THESS. 5:16-18

Whether driving to the grocery store, sitting at my computer, or cleaning my garage, my thoughts inevitably turn toward God, and I predictably sense His responses to my thoughts. Some are in the habit of kneeling when they pray. I was taught this tradition as a child, but for me, prayer does not begin when I kneel and end when I rise. It's is an ongoing conversation throughout the day. Thus, I seldom kneel when I pray. The position of my body seems to have no impact on the content or tone of my conversation with God, and it's impractical to spend the entire day kneeling. I don't believe an absence of kneeling suggests a lack of reverence. Our mind's inclination toward God is not so much a matter of our physical posture as the posture of our heart.

Intercession

You may know someone in a difficult situation that, if it continues, will not end well. When someone stands to suffer harm or death, we may not be able to intervene personally in their situation, but we can pray to God for them. *Intercession* is praying to God on behalf of another. In its simplest form, it is asking God for a change of circumstance. It may seem like a relatively safe activity, but it does involve risk.

Intercession supposes that our prayers are in the best interest of another. When we release power or exercise authority for healing sickness, there is little risk; the will of God for healing is clearly demonstrated in the ministry of Jesus, and (except in rare cases) we aren't going to make their condition worse. But the will of God for other situations is not as clear. If intercession is to be effective, it must be according to the will of God.

145

If a friend tells me they might lose their job, I could reflexively pray for them to keep it. But what if God wanted them to leave their present job so they could begin a new career? My intercessory prayer for them to remain at their current job would be contrary to the will of God. God might ignore my prayer, and my friend may lose their job. My intercession may not have hurt them, but it did not help. A better strategy would be to determine God's will for the situation and pray in agreement with it.

Imagine the same situation, but this time, let's suppose I ask God to show me what He wants for my friend. That night, I have a dream where I see my friend lose their job, but then I see them start a new career that allows them to develop a talent they'd long ignored. In this case, I would pray that God would establish His will and allow my friend to transition to the new career as painlessly as possible. I might also give my friend a prophetic word, letting them know that if they lose their job, God has a better one in mind. The key to effective intercession is knowing the mind of God and praying according to His will. Some would say it's impossible to know the mind of God, but believers have the Spirit of God living in them. We are one with God, and this allows us to know His thoughts:

> *For "who has known the mind of the Lord that he may instruct Him?" But we have the mind of Christ.*
> 1 COR. 2:16

I'm sometimes asked to pray for a person to be separated from a boyfriend, girlfriend, or spouse. These requests usually come to me through a concerned family member who believes their loved one is in a dangerous or ungodly relationship. In these cases, if I pray, I ask for God's will to be done. Since I don't know the details of the relationship or what God's desire might be, I don't want to be presumptuous. It's dangerous to pray for relationships to be severed. I'm not suggesting it should never be done, but there are risks. When we pray for a relationship to end because we believe it is harmful to someone, we're asking for *our* will to be established rather than God's. One definition of witchcraft is the desire to impose our will upon another. It's one thing to ask God to end a relationship. God may simply ignore the request. But it's another to decree that it will end using our authority.

When Elijah called down fire from heaven, lives were ruined, even though it was against God's will.

We can avoid this problem by praying in tongues. The gift of tongues is a manifestation of God's Spirit. When we pray in tongues, the Holy Spirit prays through us, and (in most cases) we speak in a language we do not understand. Because we don't know what we are saying, there is little danger of imposing our will upon another. Instead, the words we speak will be consistent with God's will.

Those who are experienced with intercession sometimes feel a burden on their heart that prompts them to pray. As long as they feel the burden, they continue in prayer. Once the burden has been lifted, they know the goal for that person or situation has been accomplished, and they can stop praying.

A similar phenomenon is reported by people who consider themselves empaths. These individuals are hypersensitive to the pains and emotions of others. At first, these experiences can seem bewildering. Empaths may initially attribute the sensations they feel to an illness. But with time and experience, they usually realize they're sensing the feelings of others. The ability to sense the pain of another can help those who are called to intercession. The sensations may change during intercession and disappear entirely once the goal of the prayers has been reached.

Petition

If I want a judge to issue a ruling on a particular legal matter, I will submit the required paperwork (usually in the form of a motion) to the appropriate court. Then, I'll appear in court on the day indicated by the clerk and present my petition to the judge, who will (hopefully) rule on my request based on the facts and the law.

A petition is a request made to someone who has the authority to grant or deny the requested action. When we ask God for a certain thing, we are petitioning Him just as we would a judge. And indeed, one of the most common titles for God found in the Bible is Judge. Our Creator is a judicial officer who presides over the highest court in the universe. We are welcome to petition Him at any time for any reason. Jesus offered a few pointers on how to petition the Father. First, He suggested that we should not pray to be seen by others as holy:

> *And when you pray, you shall not be like the hypocrites. For they love to pray standing in the synagogues and on the corners of the streets, that they may be seen by men.*
> MATT. 6:5

He instructed His disciples to pray in private and to be succinct:

> *But you, when you pray, go into your room, and when you have shut your door, pray to your Father who is in the secret place; and your Father who sees in secret will reward you openly.*
>
> *And when you pray, do not use vain repetitions as the heathen do. For they think that they will be heard for their many words.*
> MATT. 6:6-7

He told His followers to be mindful of the fact that God already knows their needs:

> *For your Father knows the things you have need of before you ask Him.*
> MATT. 6:8

You would not ask an earthly judge for permission to discipline your child. You already have that authority. In the same way, we should not ask God for that which is within our scope of authority. When we petition the Father, we should ask for that which is *outside* our scope of authority. For example, most people are in the habit of asking God for healing. But Jesus gives His followers the power and authority needed to heal the sick, even if they do not believe they have such authority.

The Apostle John offered the following observation on petitioning God:

> *Now this is the confidence that we have in Him, that if we ask anything according to His will, He hears us.*
> 1 JOHN 5:14

John highlighted two essential aspects of prayer: When we petition the Father, we should ask according to His will. This implies a knowledge of the will of God. There are general aspects to God's will that are found in scripture and specific details of His will for individuals that are revealed to us personally. Both aspects should be considered.

John wrote, "This is the *confidence* that we have in Him..." The key to receiving what we request from God is asking with confidence (faith). God grants our request when we ask in faith.

The modes of prayer we've examined in this chapter are done passively. We ask God, and He responds. The ones we'll look at next require us to be assertive. We don't ask; we *exercise the authority* God has given us.

Command

When God asked me to pray for my patients, my initial response was to petition Him to heal them. When that did not work, I eventually changed my approach and commanded broken bones, torn ligaments, and ruptured discs to be healed and commanded demons to leave. The universe responds to the kingdom of God and authoritative commands of its representatives.

Decree

A decree states the outcome of a situation in advance. Such statements should be made in accordance with the will of God. Ideally, a decree will be based on revelation we've received from the Holy Spirit. One of the most common decrees I make is that a person's doctors will determine that they have been healed of a particular disease. My statement declares the outcome in advance. Many times, the outcome is consistent with the decree.

I do not make such decrees as a matter of habit. Instead, I make them when the Holy Spirit indicates that this is the approach I should use for a particular individual. In other cases, the Holy Spirit will lead me to use a different approach.

149

When my wife is struggling to finish a painting to her complete satisfaction, I might decree that she will not only complete it but that the buyer will love it. I know God wants her to be a successful artist, and I know He has buyers in mind for her paintings. Knowing the will of God, I can decree the outcome with confidence.

Decrees can be made to change an expected outcome to one that defies logic but works in our favor. For example, I've been shopping with Denise when she wanted to go to a particular store after it would normally be closed. After making a decree that the store would remain open, we arrived after hours to find them open for business. It's not unusual for us to spend time going from one store to another looking for a specific item. On occasion, I've decreed that she would find the item she was looking for at a particular store, and a few minutes later, she found the exact item she was seeking.

Up to this point, we've discussed the issues over which all believers have authority. Although God grants broad authority to us as a group, each individual is granted authority over particular issues. The individual's scope of authority will be discussed in the next section.

CHAPTER TWENTY-FOUR

Re-arming the Saints

A FEW YEARS AGO, IN a dream, I saw a factory where body parts were being assembled to create humans. During assembly, people were assigned a six-digit numerical code, which indicated what body parts they would receive during assembly. But there was a problem. The codes that had been assigned to some people were incorrect. And as a result of receiving the wrong codes, some people had been given the wrong type of arms. I was involved in correcting the misassembled individuals. Based on what I knew about their calling, gifting, and the types of arms that were available, I was tasked with re-arming them.

The dream referred to my calling as one of "arming" the body of Christ. When I think of "arms," I often think of spiritual weapons, equipping, and training. That language is found in the Apostle Paul's letter to the church in Ephesus, where he explained the purpose for various positions of leadership:

And He Himself gave some to be apostles, some prophets, some evangelists, and some pastors and teachers, for the equipping of the saints for the work of ministry, for the edifying of the body of Christ.
EPH. 4:11-12

In the dream, the codes that had been assigned to individuals had six digits. In the Bible, the number six represents a number of man. Adam was created on the sixth day (see Gen. 26-31). The book of Revelation also associates the number six with man:

Here is wisdom. Let him who has understanding calculate the number of the beast, for it is the number of a man: His number is 666.
REV. 13:18

People were assigned the wrong codes (by other humans). As a result, they received the wrong arms. Symbolically, arms refer to weapons of spiritual warfare. I would interpret this as an indication that errors have been made by spiritual leaders who have misidentified the equipping their followers need. I'm not certain how leaders have misidentified the training and equipping needs of their followers, but I do have a hunch. It's common for a leader to want followers to operate in the same type of calling they do. What father doesn't want his son to take up the family business? The value we place on an issue is personal. When we value something highly, we sometimes project our value onto others. Pastors desire to train and equip more pastors. The same is true for evangelists and prophets. I suspect that herein lies the problem.

I once knew a man who pastored a small church. He seemed to have little passion for the job, but he became excited and energized whenever he traveled outside the U.S. to do the work of an evangelist. In talking with others who knew him, it was obvious that he was called to be an evangelist. Yet, he never fully embraced that calling. Instead, he settled for a job as a pastor, an unfulfilling role that had probably been assigned to him by another pastor.

This man's ministry is an example of how we can mistakenly accept a position to which we are not called. There are many reasons why we make such compromises. Convenience, fear of what others might think, fear of failure, and fear of financial ruin are but a few. The solution proposed in the dream was to re-arm people based on what was known about their true calling, their true gifting, and the arms that were available. Re-arming (in this context) is a matter of suggesting to others ways they might correct poor choices.

The question of how one can effectively correct someone is a thorny issue. For years, I've avoided trying to correct others. Often, my attempts were a waste of time. I have no interest in giving advice that is not heeded. Many times, the individual we wish to help cannot or will not receive correction. Before one can effectively correct another, they must establish a relationship of mutual trust and respect. We can, of course, speak correction to anyone we want, and many of us do, but correction from a stranger is seldom heeded. That type of correction bears no fruit and may create bitterness, mistrust, and resentment. A relationship of mutual trust and respect allows one to speak words of correction to another in a way that will be received. Only when correction is received will it bear fruit.

The calling and gifting of others are matters that require God's counsel. Once trust has been established, we can ask God what position a person is called to and what type of gifts they have that will help them operate in their calling. Training and equipping them for their calling is a matter of understanding how the weapons of spiritual warfare operate, how the strategies and tactics of ministry function and how they aid us in operating in our spheres of authority.

If a friend is authorized to be a prophet, we will do well to encourage them to develop their ability to see visions, receive words of knowledge and words of wisdom. Prophets are people of revelation, and these tools help them operate in their calling. If they're authorized as an evangelist, we might help them receive training in healing and miracles, as healing and evangelism make a powerful combination. Leaders who correctly discern the gifting, calling, and weaponry needed for others, and who can assist in their development, are invaluable resources to the body of Christ.

CHAPTER TWENTY-FIVE

Obedience to God

WISDOM DICTATES THAT AUTHORITY SHOULD be exercised in a way that is consistent with God's nature and plans. The goal is exercising authority in obedience. And that begs the question: what exactly is obedience to God? Every sermon I've heard that addressed obedience to God equated it with adherence to a moral code of conduct. As much as new covenant teachers emphasize God's grace toward our transgressions, it's difficult to break the habit of observing our own moral conduct with concern. I don't think obedience is best described as adherence to a moral code. True obedience to God is a deeper issue. I would propose that obedience is a matter of coming into agreement with Him. But agreement over what?

God's primary concern toward Adam and Eve wasn't their adherence to a moral code. He wanted a loving relationship with them. Their relationship wasn't ruined because of disobedience. Consider for a moment what would have happened if Adam had eaten from the forbidden tree but continued to embrace God as his loving Father. He would still have disobeyed a moral code, but his disobedience would not have destroyed his relationship with God. Their relationship was damaged not when he disobeyed, but when he forgot that he was deeply loved and he hid from God. The enemy's chief tactic has always been to call into question God's affection for us—to suggest that we are not loved and that we are not His child. The real trick the enemy pulled that day was not convincing Adam to disobey God. It was convincing him that God didn't love him. The enemy uses the same tactic today.

When Satan tempted Jesus in the wilderness for 40 days, one trick he deployed was questioning the identity of the Son of God. The tactic failed because Jesus knew exactly who He was and how much the Father loved Him, despite the suffering He endured.

How many of us have avoided drawing closer to God out of fear that He may reject us? If your parents rejected you or seldom showed affection, you might incorrectly think that God sees you the same way.

Sin is a problem, but it results from our failure to understand who we are. It's not merely an issue of obeying a moral code. It's a matter of identity. All our efforts to avoid sin will not free us from moral failure. But when we fully grasp the reality of our identity as beloved children of God—and when we live from that identity—sin no longer has power over us.

Most believers know they are children of God in some sense of the word. But for some, this knowledge amounts to little more than intellectual agreement with an idea. Many have adopted something else as their *functional* identity–the identity from which they operate.

For some, the role of a mother is their functional identity. Others have taken their job title or favorite hobby as their identity. When you ask them who they are, they reply that they're a stockbroker, a nurse, a mother, or a race car driver. The identity that we hold highest above all others is the one from which the issues of life flow. Adopting a job title as our identity can have severe consequences. When we identify ourselves by our occupation and enter retirement, we no longer function in that identity. A lost sense of identity can lead to depression and even suicide.

When you find someone who, without knowing your agenda, answers the question "Who are you?" with something like, "I'm an ambassador of the King of heaven" or "I am a son of God," you've found someone who has adopted their true identity in Christ. Such a person will find it easy to exercise authority and release power.

Our identity helps us fulfill our divine destiny. The identities the world imposes on us can replace our divine identity. When we take on a false identity, we pursue the wrong destiny. The positions we're given in life may supplant the identity God has given us. We should carefully consider whether the identities and positions we've accepted from the world are in harmony with the identity, destiny, and authority given to us by God.

I once saw myself as a worthless sinner, albeit one who had been saved by grace. That was the identity I had accepted. I never saw anyone healed when I saw myself this way. It took about a year to make the mental transition from that identity to seeing myself as a beloved and empowered child of God. Once I accepted my true identity, I witnessed miracles regularly. The change in my identity brought about a change in the way I impacted the world around me.

Obedience to God is perhaps best understood as fully agreeing with everything He says about us. It's embracing our true identity and destiny and accepting that we are unconditionally loved and wholly accepted by our heavenly Father. That reality should make obeying God a joy and not a chore. When we receive instruction from Him, knowing that He has our best interest in mind, we can carry out His instructions with zeal.

CHAPTER TWENTY-SIX

Are You Authorized?

EACH ONE OF US HAS BEEN granted authority from God in several areas. If you're a parent, you have authority over your child and how they are raised. You have authority over your fields and livestock if you're a farmer. If you're a Christian, you're authorized to share the good news of the kingdom with others.

While it's helpful to know the specific subjects over which Jesus has given us authority, it's also good to know the areas over which He has *not* given us authority and what consequences we can expect when we involve ourselves in matters outside our scope of authority.

A few years ago, I had a dream where Jesus came to the church to check the credentials of those who taught others about God. Those who taught without authorization from Him were in trouble. The primary issue of concern was *authorization*. A secondary issue was the content that was being taught. Many false ideas about God were spread by people who weren't authorized by Jesus. In the dream, the fact that they needed to be authorized to speak on certain subjects surprised most people. Social networks have created a global platform where anyone who wants to share their opinions about God can find an audience. You don't have to look very far to see people publicly preaching their ideas about what or whom God loves or hates. We're bombarded with theological opinions around the clock, and apparently, Jesus is listening.

I've discovered that Jesus is conscious of the things that I say. The topics about which I'm authorized to speak as His representative are limited. I'm authorized to speak on healing, deliverance, prophetic ministry, dreams, current events, and a few other subjects. I have opinions about matters such as tithing, the rapture, and abortion. I believe I know what the Bible says about these issues, and I could offer my views on them, but God hasn't authorized me to speak on these matters and He hasn't given me specific revelations about them. I know that His authorization carries with it His revelation. The issues God shares with me, I'm willing to share with others. But topics about which He is silent (to me) are ones I do not address publicly. I want to operate within my scope of authority.

One of the difficulties with authority is that in addition to permitting us to speak on certain issues, it restrains us from speaking on others. Jesus modeled this restraint by only saying what the Father authorized Him to say and doing what the Father allowed Him to do.

> *"Most assuredly, I say to you, the Son can do nothing of Himself, but what He sees the Father do; for whatever He does, the Son also does in like manner.*
> JOHN 5:19

> *For I have not spoken on My own authority; but the Father who sent Me gave Me a command, what I should say and what I should speak.*
> JOHN 12:49

The proper exercise of authority requires discipline and self-control. Due to our unique personalities, gifts, talents, and life experiences, God authorizes each of us differently. If He has called you to be a painter, He'll inspire your art and provide an attentive audience. If He has gifted you to be a chef, He'll give you an understanding of the best ways to prepare food and plenty of hungry patrons. Those who have been authorized to speak on a particular subject are given God's heart on that matter, the necessary life experiences, a means of conveying their message, and an audience with ears to hear it.

Having God's authorization to speak on a subject creates a favorable environment. Those who speak on issues He has authorized tend to bear good fruit. Those who speak without His authorization generally bear poor fruit.

I'm often asked questions about matters that God has not authorized me to address. A recent example is vaccines. While I know people who have received personal revelation from God on that subject, I can't think of anything He has revealed to me about that issue. So, when people ask for my thoughts on vaccines, I tell them, "I have no revelation on that," and point them to someone who has. There's no shame in admitting ignorance on a particular issue. However, if you give people counsel that isn't from God, you'll lead them astray. Therefore, it's wiser to say nothing about subjects we're not authorized to address. In the following chapters, I'll share insights about how I found my divine destiny and how that discovery helped me understand the areas in which God has authorized me.

Exercise

Ask Jesus what subjects you are and are not authorized to speak on and make a list of topics. Once you have the list, ask Him to reveal His heart on those issues and confine your conversations to those subjects on which He has authorized you to speak.

CHAPTER TWENTY-SEVEN

To Every Messenger, a Message

WHAT FOLLOWS IS A BIT of personal instruction God gave me that allows me to see my efforts the way He sees them. It may help you see your efforts the same way.

While every believer has the same King, and we're all asked to bear witness of Him to the world, how we do it is unique. We're all given messages from God to deliver to others. Some of us are called to be evangelists, some writers, some pastors, and others are called to repair cars, or teach their children about Jesus.

For years, I struggled with knowing how to effectively share the good new about Jesus. Then, one night, God said to me, "I'll show you what's wrong with your patients. You pray, and I'll heal them." I'd wager that none of the eight billion people on earth have received that same message. You have messages from God that are unique, just as mine are unique. Every believer has a set of messages to deliver, and every message has an audience.

God has given me all kinds of messages; many come through dreams and visions. When I receive one, I write it down in a journal. Since most of my messages come in the form of symbolic imagery and abstract concepts, they must be decoded. The Holy Spirit helps me interpret these messages into a language that can be understood. I post them in articles and videos on my website. Anyone interested can access them at their convenience. Those who read those posts and watch the videos are the audience God has provided. Some people post their messages to a website, as I do; your process may be unique to you.

When I write an article, I limit myself to only those subjects God has authorized me to address. When we obediently deliver only the messages He gives us to the audience He provides, those who hear us are likely to receive our messages and bear good fruit. When I want to provide my audience with a message I haven't received from God, I recruit someone else to deliver *their* message on *my* website or podcast. In this way, I provide messages on a variety of topics without going outside the authorization and revelation God has given me.

My messages have critics who occasionally post negative comments. Thankfully, God showed me how to deal with them. In a dream, I saw people leaving comments on the articles I posted. Most of the comments were positive, but a few were negative. In the dream, I knew I had to keep posting my messages for the sake of those who benefited from them. I didn't let the critics get me down, and neither should you.

How do we know what subjects God has authorized us to address?

Sometimes, the issues for which we have authority are cloaked in our passion for a topic. Generally, your messages will be related to the things God mentions in your conversations with Him. He does not always dictate the subject matter of these conversations. I've been surprised at how talkative He can be and how much instruction He'll provide about issues I've brought up. Some of the information I've received has been for my benefit only. I don't always obtain permission to speak on these subjects publicly.

Knowing which subjects you've been authorized to speak about publicly (and which you haven't) is critical to reaching the audience God has prepared for each message. Your adherence to this instruction will determine whether your messages bear fruit. While it's tempting to speak on an issue out of our understanding from personal experience, it's best to speak from revelation we've received directly from God. He can tailor our message so that it addresses the issue from His perspective, expresses His heart, and positively impacts the audience that He has prepared for us.

There are many subjects that we may be authorized to address. Whether we have permission to speak on a particular issue does not make it any more or less important to God. We should avoid thinking that a matter is less significant to Him because He has not authorized us to address it.

Have you ever delivered the right message to the wrong audience? I have many friends who spend hours in heated debates on social media because they haven't realized that their message is not intended for a universal audience. They believe everyone must hear a particular message, but in reality, God has prepared the hearts of only a few people who can receive a particular message and bear fruit from it.

The two keys to bearing good fruit as a messenger are knowing your message, and recognizing its intended audience. Generally, you know you've found an audience with ears to hear when your message is received well by those who hear it. That's not to say we should never expect resistance if we deliver a message to its intended audience. A skeptic, who is part of the intended audience, may initially resist your message. God may try to persuade them to consider a different point of view through the discussion. Over time, their heart may soften, and they may be able to receive your message. But if you're routinely met with hostility, rejection, and quarreling, you may need to re-evaluate your message or the audience you're trying to reach. The apostle Paul thought he was called to preach to the Jews, but God's intended audience for him was the Gentiles. He had the right message but delivered it to the wrong audience.

I don't know what messages you're called to deliver, and I don't know your audience. That's between you and God. I would encourage you to ask Him for the messages He wants you to deliver. Once you have a message, trust that He will provide an audience who will receive it— no matter how small it might be. Some are called to speak to millions, some to thousands, and others, to only a handful of people. The size of your audience isn't important. What matters is your obedience to God. If you obey His instruction, your message will bear good fruit.

CHAPTER TWENTY-EIGHT

Finding Your Destiny

A FRIEND SENT ME AN email one day after I appeared to her in her dream. She asked what the best way was to get people healed. I told her, "It's all about your mojo." She wanted to know if I could explain that.

Not the healing thing. The mojo thing.

After I published my first book, *Divine Healing Made Simple,* some of my friends who also taught healing were invited to speak at a conference. I was invited too, but I wasn't able to attend. Because I worked full-time as a paramedic, I could not take the required time off. The conference I missed began a season where I struggled with melancholy. My peers in healing soon began traveling around the country, speaking at more conferences while I worked my job. I was happy for them. They were teaching cutting-edge topics that people needed to learn. Still, I couldn't help but feel sorry for myself.

One day, I had a discussion with the Holy Spirit. I asked Him an uncomfortable question: "When am I going to have my chance?"

"Is that what you want?" He replied.

"I don't know. I've never tried it."

There were certainly doubts in my mind about whether the life of an itinerant minister was for me. I was 30 years into a medical career, and throwing it all away so I could speak on the church conference circuit seemed a bit impulsive. Still, I felt overlooked. But there were bills to pay and books to write, so I focused my attention on writing.

Not long after this, my wife had a dream. In the dream, she went to buy a Christmas tree and ended up at the house of C.S. Lewis' parents. They had a tree for sale and told her all about it. They also told her about something else that was for sale—their son's writing desk. The desk and the Christmas tree were being sold for the same price. My wife could only buy one.

I love C.S Lewis. Although he had an effective ministry, he didn't travel the way itinerant preachers and evangelists do. He influenced the world from behind his writing desk. I understood the symbolism of the desk, but I did not understand the symbolism of the Christmas tree. That revelation would come later.

I kept working on the ambulance and wrote a couple more books. My friends continued speaking at conferences and church meetings. Then one day, I was given my chance.

The conference I was asked to speak at was the perfect venue for someone like myself. It was small. There were lots of friends in attendance. And I was surrounded by mature ministers with whom I could share the platform. I wouldn't be the center of attention. "The Gathering," as we called it, was perfect in another way.

A friend was there who was more developed in his gifting, and he was willing to minister to the audience. My friend Steve Harmon spent the weekend praying and prophesying over people and setting them free of past trauma. That allowed me time to mingle with my friends. The closest I came to doing any real "ministry" was hanging out with Steve while he did his thing. Although I enjoyed my time at The Gathering, I felt moments of discomfort being in the spotlight.

A couple of months later, I was asked to speak at a church in the Midwest. The pastor said many well-known ministers had spoken there recently, and he thought I would be a good fit. I asked what I would be expected to do. He explained that I would give a couple of messages to the audience, pray for people to be healed, deliver prophetic words, and walk away with financial compensation. I always pray and ask God to direct me when I get an offer like this, but truthfully, I was not feeling drawn to it.

It isn't that I don't like these meetings. I love being in God's presence and seeing miracles. It's not that I don't like people; I'm an extrovert in every sense of the word. I like praying for people, although long days at conferences can be emotionally draining and physically exhausting. The larger problem is the disruption to my schedule that happens when I travel.

I generally like traveling for pleasure. But I could not imagine living half my life out of a suitcase where the routine consists of attending meetings, praying for strangers, going to bed every night exhausted, and knowing that I need to get up early to catch another plane. Is there time on the way to the airport to grab a cup of coffee?

I like my daily routine, but can't follow it when traveling. Most days, I wake up early without an alarm. The first order of business is making coffee. If I'm in the mood, I'll make breakfast. Denise and I chat about our plans for the day as we watch the sunrise, listen to the birds in the palm trees and enjoy our view of the patio from our living room. Then, I'll check my email and answer prayer requests. When that is done, I turn my attention to writing.

Most days, I sit at my desk with a cup of coffee and write. I might work on a new article, research a supernatural subject, or edit the manuscript for a book. It's a routine, and it may sound boring. But it's my routine, and I'm addicted to it. There's nothing I love more than writing. I love it, perhaps, because it's where I encounter God. We all encounter God in different ways. When I write, I feel as if He's sitting next to me. I ask Him questions. He shares His thoughts. I sit at my computer and dictate our conversations. It's how I've come to know Him and how He's working out my destiny. And it happens to be my favorite form of worship.

One of the most important things you'll ever discover is your divine destiny. Although there are general purposes for which man was created, there are unique reasons why each person is brought into the world. Your divine destiny is the unique set of purposes for which God has created you.

We were created for His good pleasure. Part of His pleasure is watching us grow into the person He has designed us to be and do the things He destined us to do. While it's true that we are human "beings" and not human "doings," what we "do" in this life does matter.

Your destiny is closely tied to the passions of your heart—the things you desire more than anything else. God is the one who gives us the desires of our hearts, and they're given for a reason. They motivate and propel us toward our divinely ordained destiny.

We often let obstacles like time and money prevent us from pursuing our destiny. One person's destiny might involve being a painter, but if they believe that painting won't pay the bills, they may forego their destiny and settle for a job as a graphic designer. One person's destiny might be an author, but they may think they'll never have the time to finish their first book, and if they do, no one will buy it. Fear prevents us from pursuing our destiny. Fear is empowered by our belief in the lie that we can't make a living doing it or we'll never have the time to develop our skills.

Shortly after I turned 50, I stopped believing the lie that I couldn't make a living as a writer. My greatest passion is writing. It probably always has been, though I suppressed my desire to write for most of my life. I never thought I could make a living as an author, so for more than three decades, I made a living as a paramedic. Then, after a series of conversations with Denise, I decided to spend my free time pursuing a career as a writer. She saw just as clearly my destiny as a writer as I saw hers as a painter. The more I pursued what God created me to do, the more time and resources He made available. As I came into alignment with my divine assignment, the favor of God increased on what I was doing. Today, I'm living out my destiny. I write for a living, and I love every minute of it.

Being a writer isn't a flashy life. There's no podium. No bright lights. It's not sparkly and shiny like the Christmas tree in my wife's dream. But it's comfortable. And if you happen to be a writer, it's one of the things God has authorized you to do. God knew I wasn't cut out to be an itinerant minister. So, He gave me a wife who believed in me and gave her a dream.

God has a unique plan for you. A unique destiny. A unique sphere of authority. Your destiny doesn't look like mine. When you see someone who has found their mojo, don't be envious. Be glad. They've discovered their destiny. If someone tries to hand you a destiny that isn't a good fit, don't settle for it. God's plan for you is perfect. Hold out for the one thing that's comfortable. The thing that fits you like a glove. When you find it, you'll know it. Until then, keep asking and seeking. Your destiny is out there looking for you.

Exercise

How does a person discover their divine destiny?

To remove fear from the equation, ask yourself what you would do if time and money were no object. What would you do with the rest of your life if you had all the resources you needed and all the time in the world? Ask yourself what one thing gets you excited. It's likely that this one thing is tied to your divine destiny. If there is some career you can name that involves this thing—this passion, consider pursuing it and see if God doesn't open a few doors for you.

INKITY
PRESS™

Other books from Praying Medic

For up-to-date titles go to: PrayingMedic.com

Series—The Kingdom of God Made Simple:

Divine Healing Made Simple
Seeing in the Spirit Made Simple
Hearing God's Voice Made Simple
Traveling in the Spirit Made Simple
Dream Interpretation Made Simple
Power and Authority Made Simple

Series—My Craziest Adventures with God:

My Craziest Adventures with God - Volume 1
My Craziest Adventures with God - Volume 2

Series—The Courts of Heaven:

Defeating Your Adversary in the Court of Heaven
Operating in the Court of Angels

And more:

Emotional Healing in 3 Easy Steps
The Gates of Shiloh (a novel)
God Speaks: Perspectives on Hearing God's Voice (28 authors)
A Kingdom View of Economic Collapse (eBook only)
American Sniper: Lessons in Spiritual Warfare (eBook only)

SCAN THIS TO GO TO
PrayingMedic.com

Made in the USA
Coppell, TX
01 September 2023